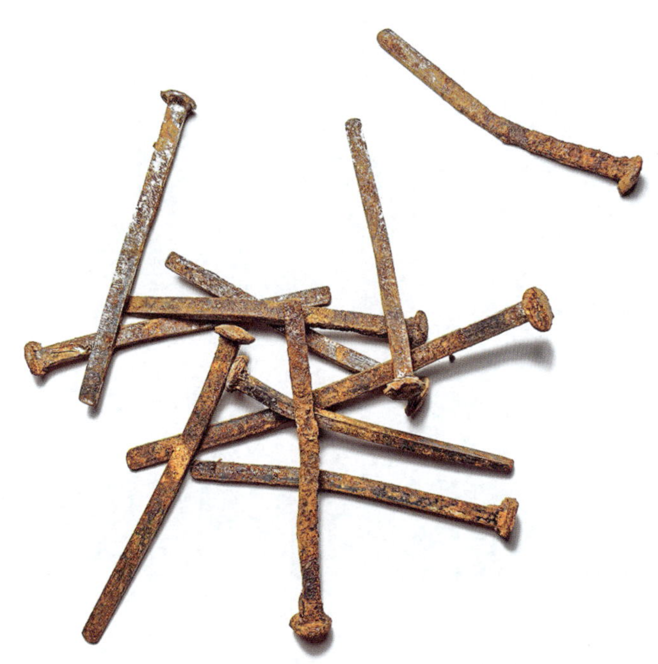

Bears All Things

Mammu & Pasi Rauhala

KERBER PHOTO

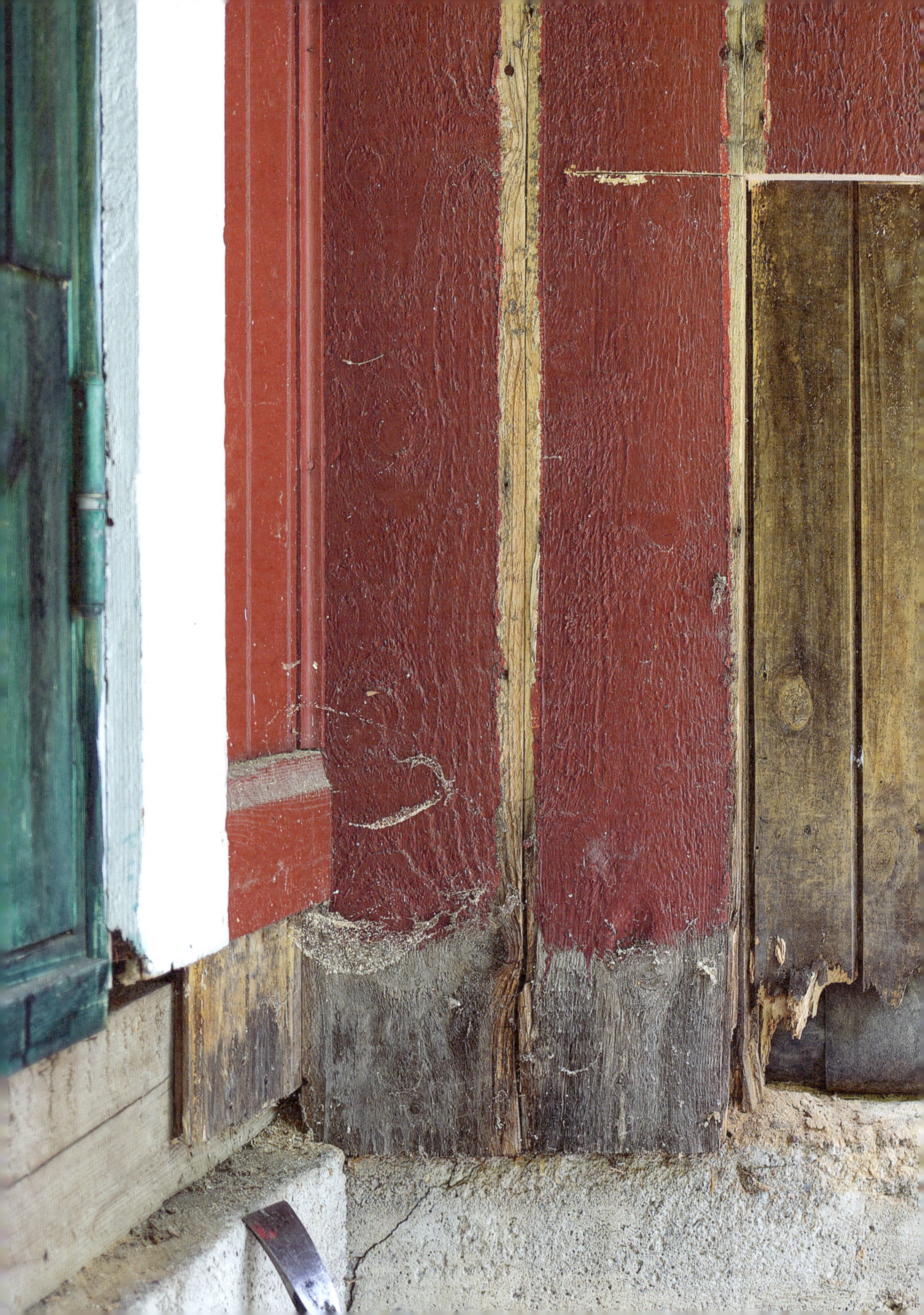

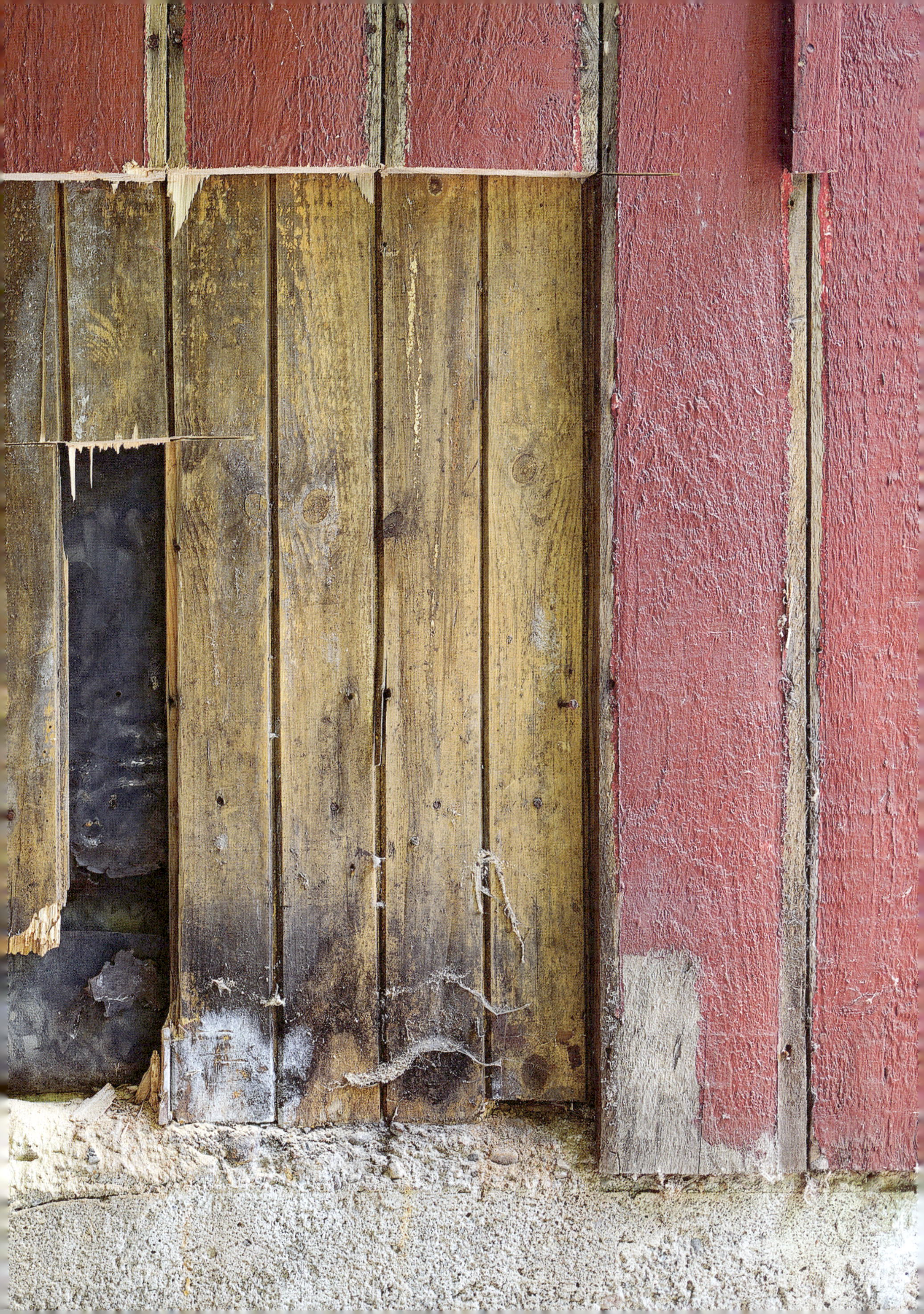

Preface

Dear Reader,

You are holding a book that tells you a story about our everyday life in our old log house. This house is a scene of work, time, joy, love, and commitment. We don't exactly know when the house was originally built, but it has stood at this site since at least the 1930s providing many working class families and lonely grannies a roof over their heads.

Through this book we invite you to our home. You can see glimpses of our life and time passing by. *Bears All Things* (originally in Finnish 'Kaiken se kestää') is a lifelong art project where we document our daily lives wearing wedding attires. The undertaking, which began in 2013, has been carried out annually. The works explore time, humanity, and interpersonal relationships. A vital component of the oeuvre is the photographs in which we stare at the camera with a serious look on our faces while wearing our wedding outfits. Over the years, the work has also evolved in its form to include a video installation, a performance, and a sculpture. In addition to *Bears All Things*, other correlative series have emerged—focusing on issues related to love and its preservation.

The themes of change and permanence as well as daily life and merriment, are in dialogue. The world is changing, and so are our perceptions of home and our relationship with each other. Our art celebrates the daily decision to accept change together.

We're glad you found the three of us,
Mammu, Pasi and the House

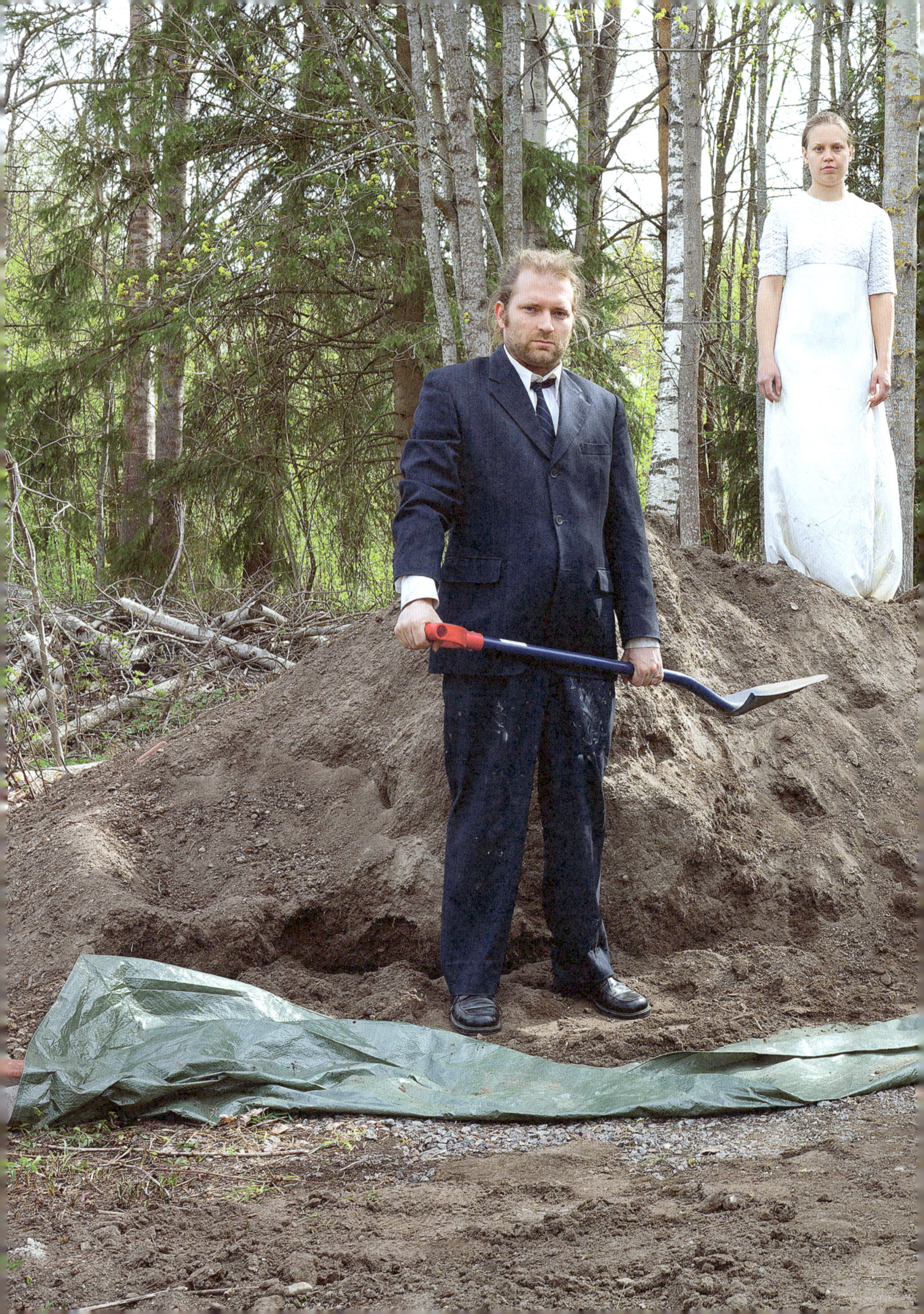

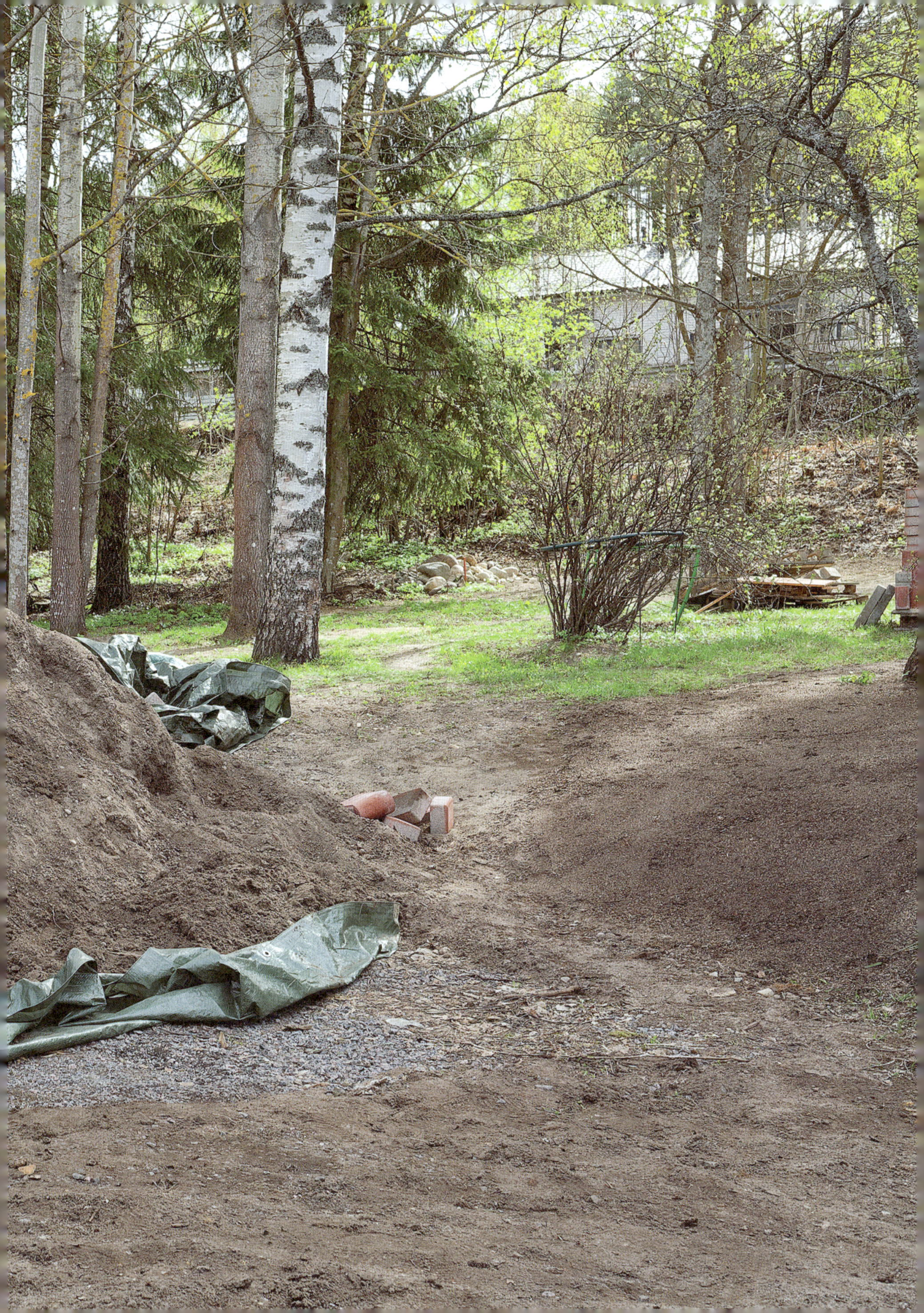

The House

A Short Story by Mammu with AI

In a quiet Finnish town, where time whispered secrets in every breeze, there stood an old and stubborn House. It had weathered the years with a touch of defiance, bearing the marks of neglect and the weight of its own history. As the seasons danced by, the House remained steadfast, its weary frame yearning for respite.

…

...

When the young couple arrived, their hearts filled with determination and a hunger for transformation, the House bristled with resistance. It groaned in protest, as if to say, "Enough! Haven't I endured enough already?" The couple's optimistic visions of renovation clashed with the House's weariness, setting the stage for an arduous battle of wills.

...

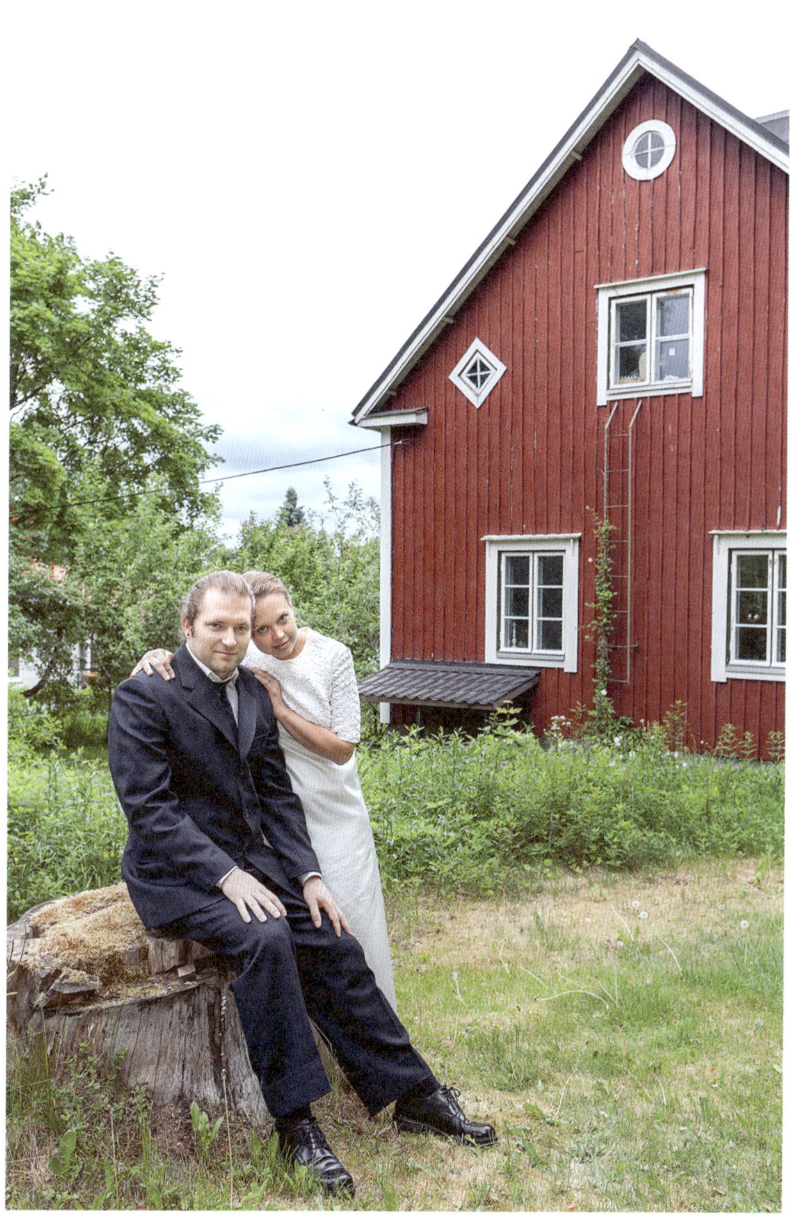

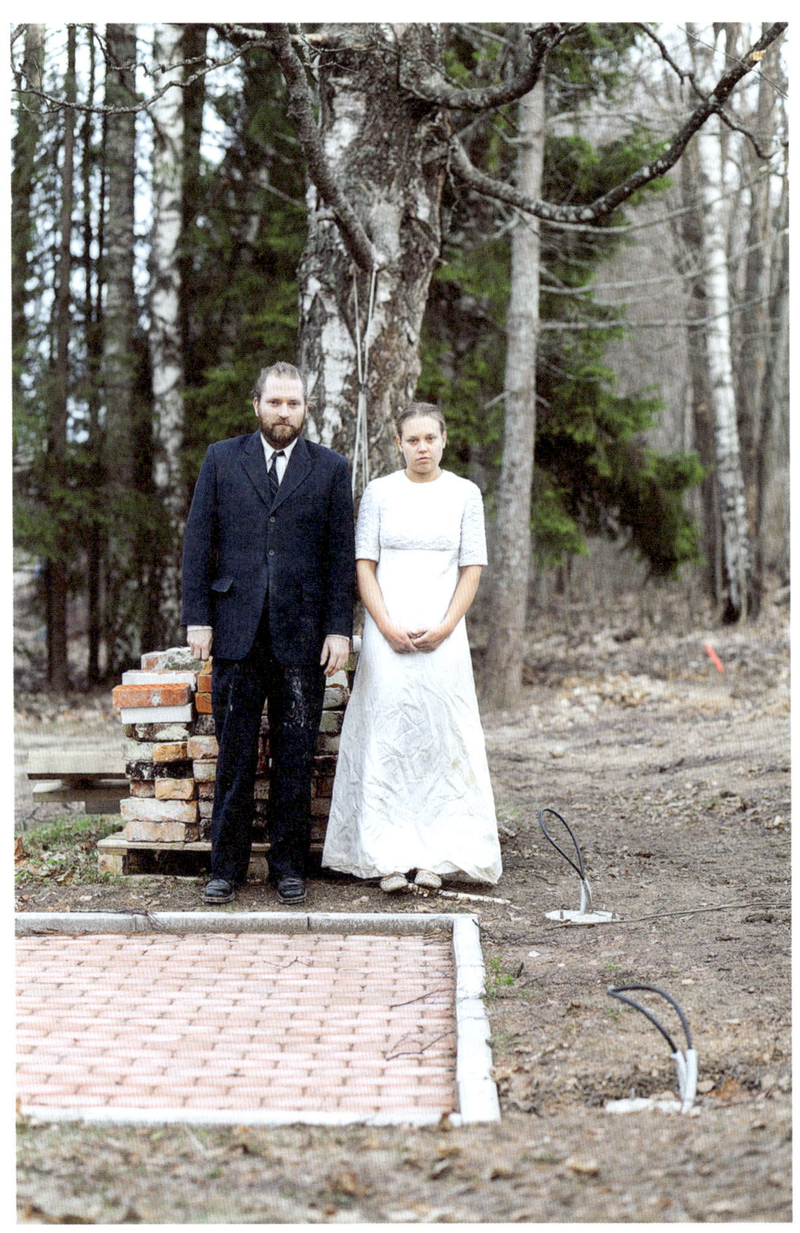

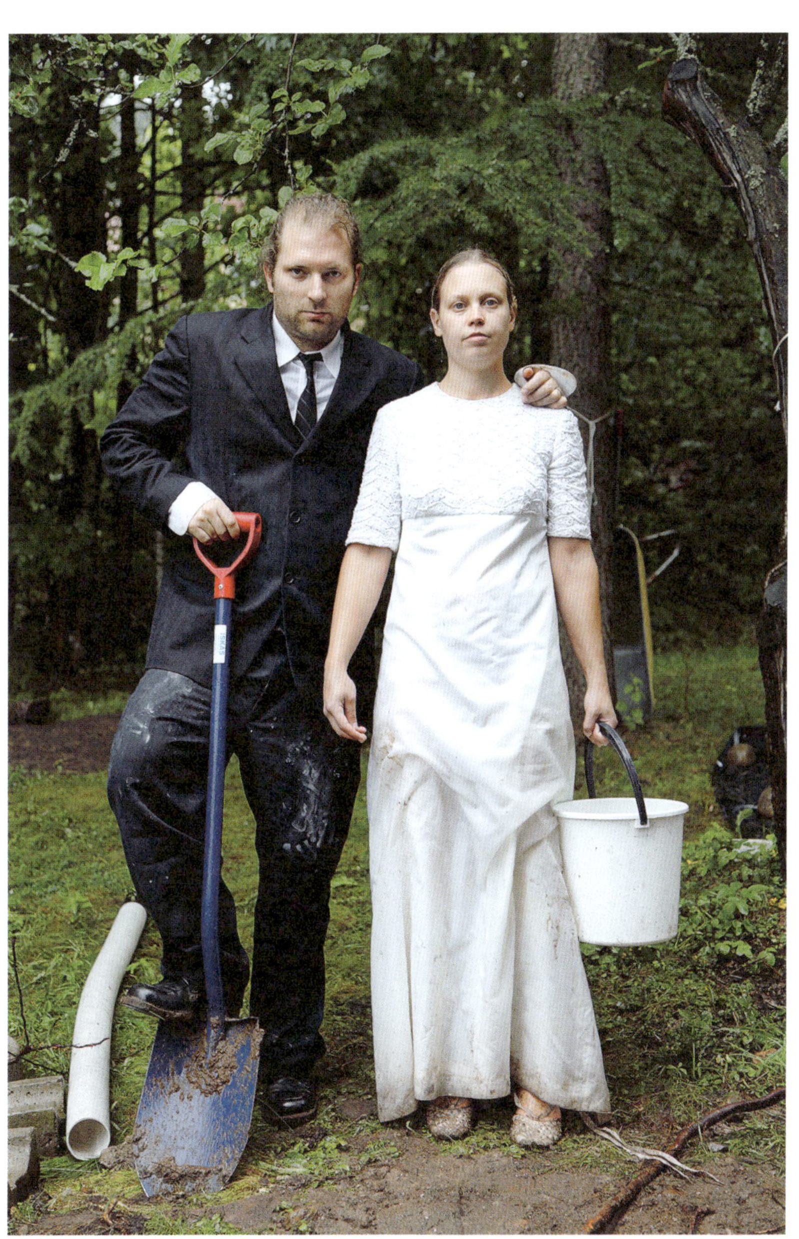

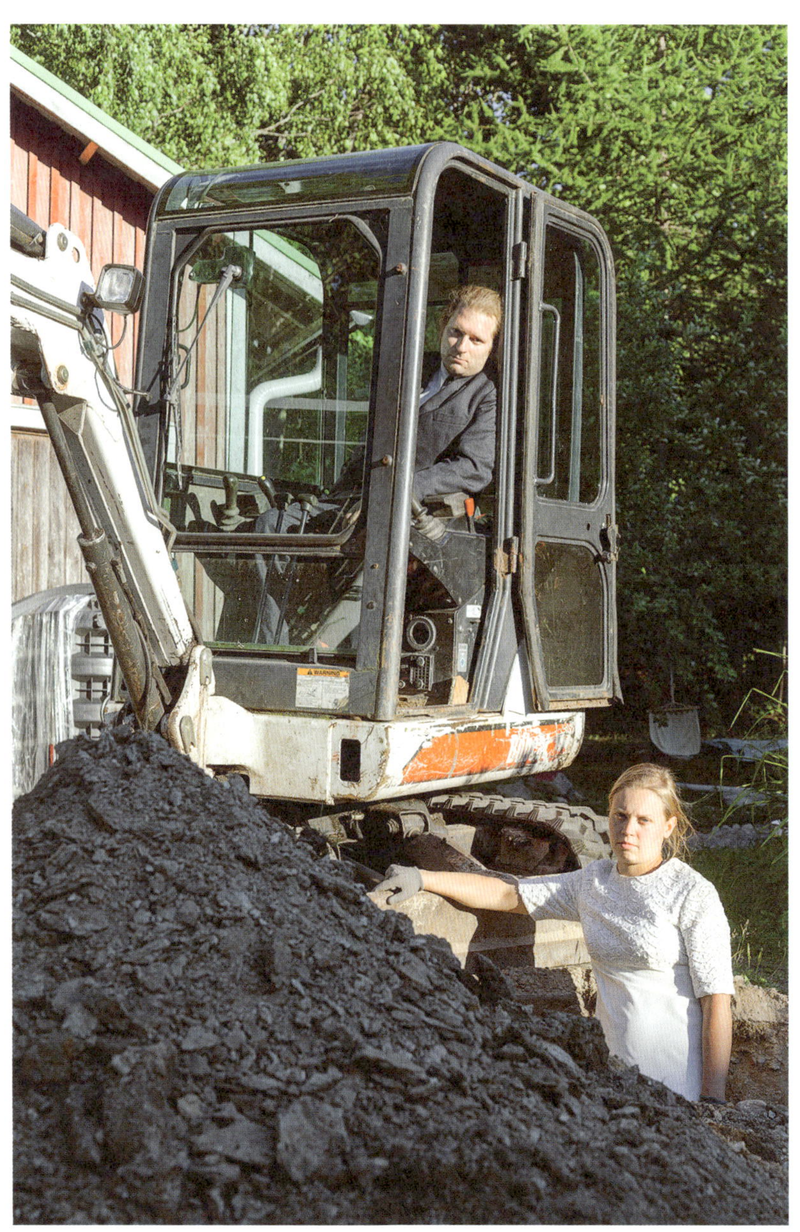

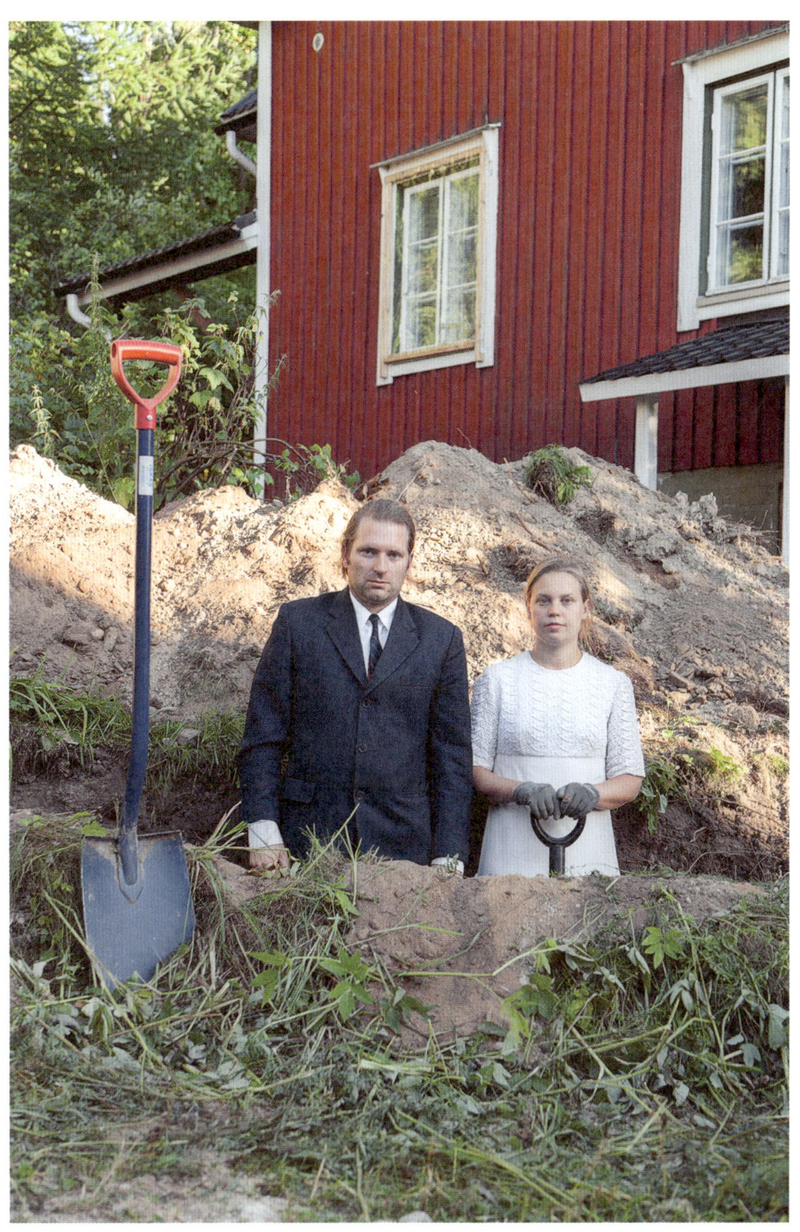

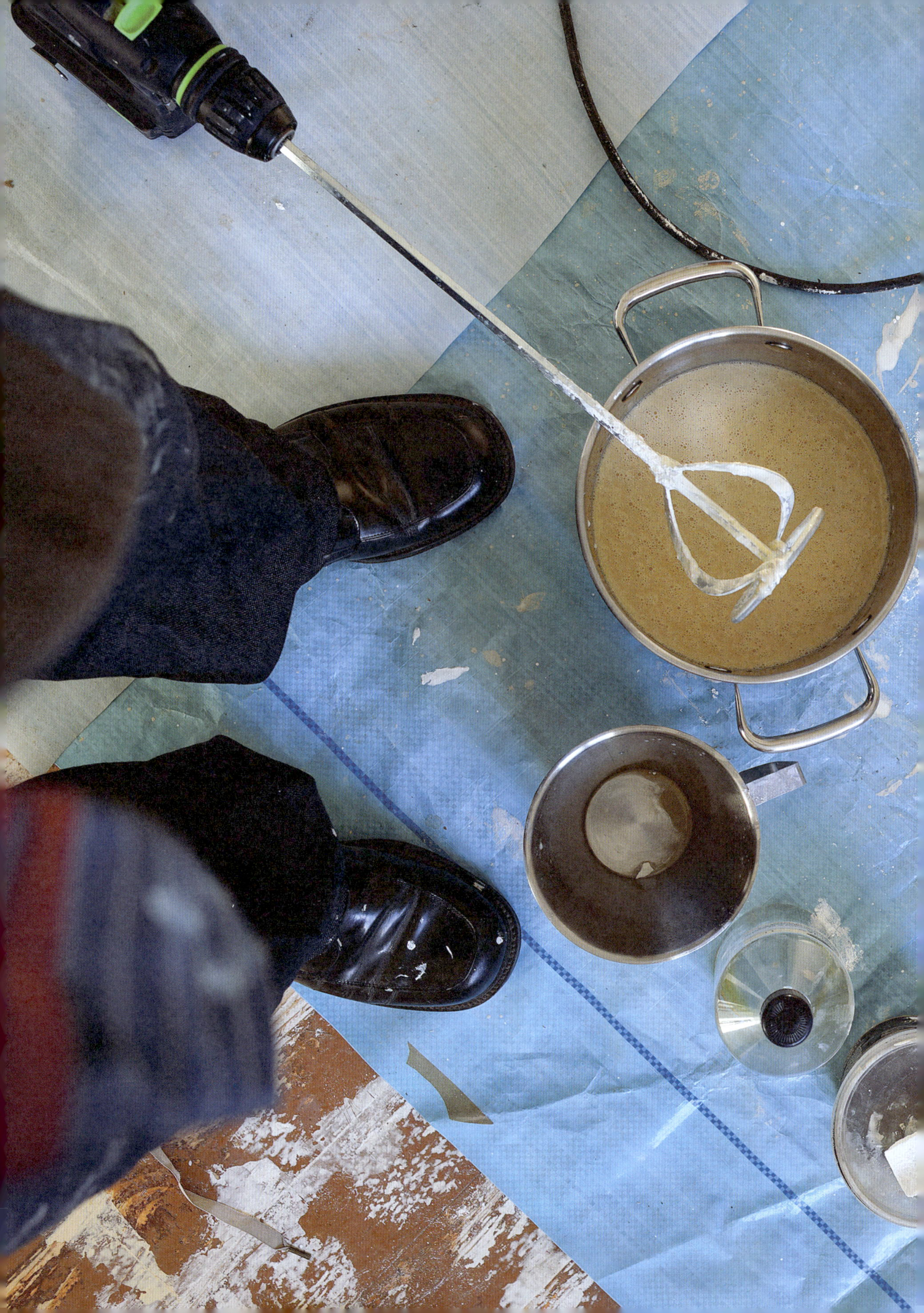

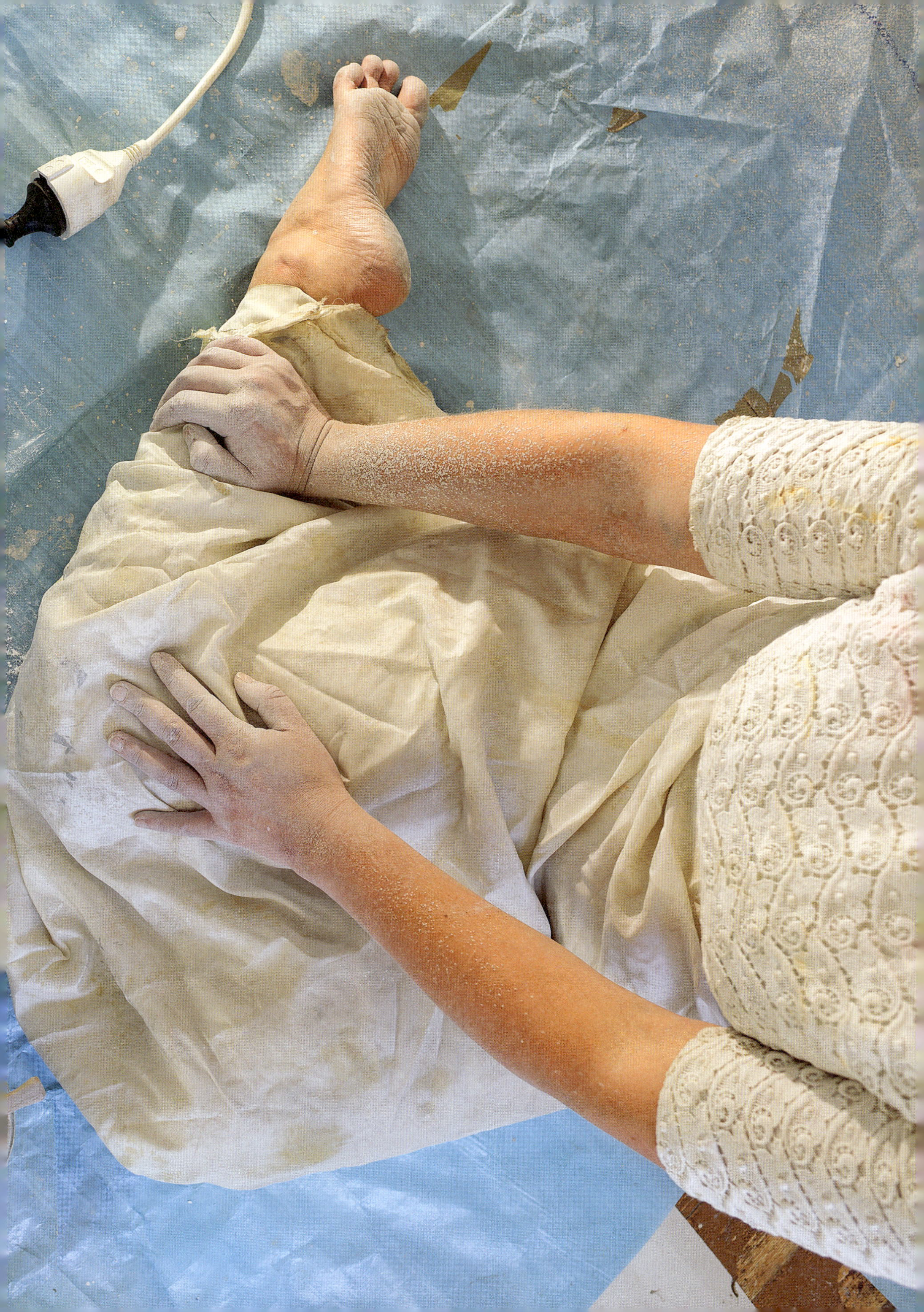

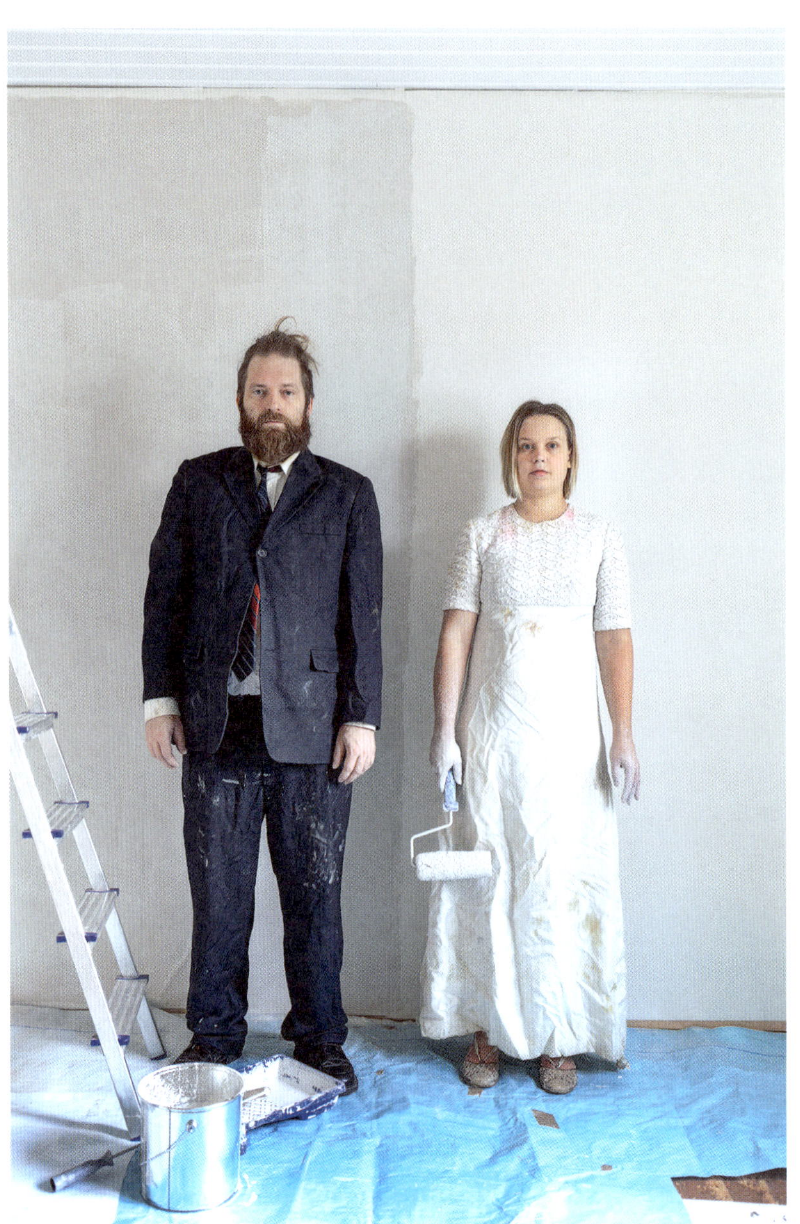

...

Undeterred by the House's grumpy disposition, the couple rolled up their sleeves and delved into the sea of renovations. They labored tirelessly, painting over the faded walls, replacing worn floorboards, and breathing life into forgotten corners. But no matter how much they repaired and rejuvenated, the House seemed insatiable, forever hungry for more.

...

...

As each project neared its completion, the House's discontent grew. It resisted their efforts, causing pipes to leak and walls to crack, as if to test their resolve. The couple, worn but unyielding, refused to be deterred. They saw beyond the House's grumpy facade, recognizing the potential within its timeworn walls.

...

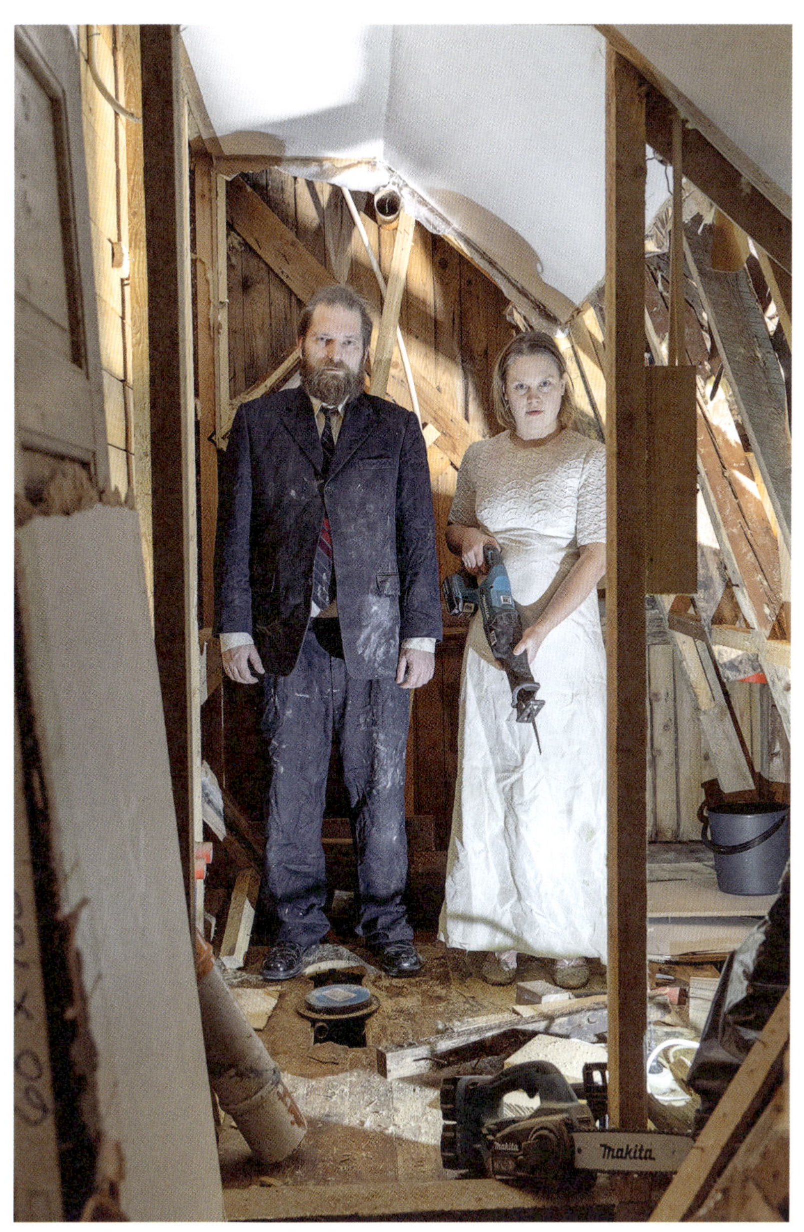

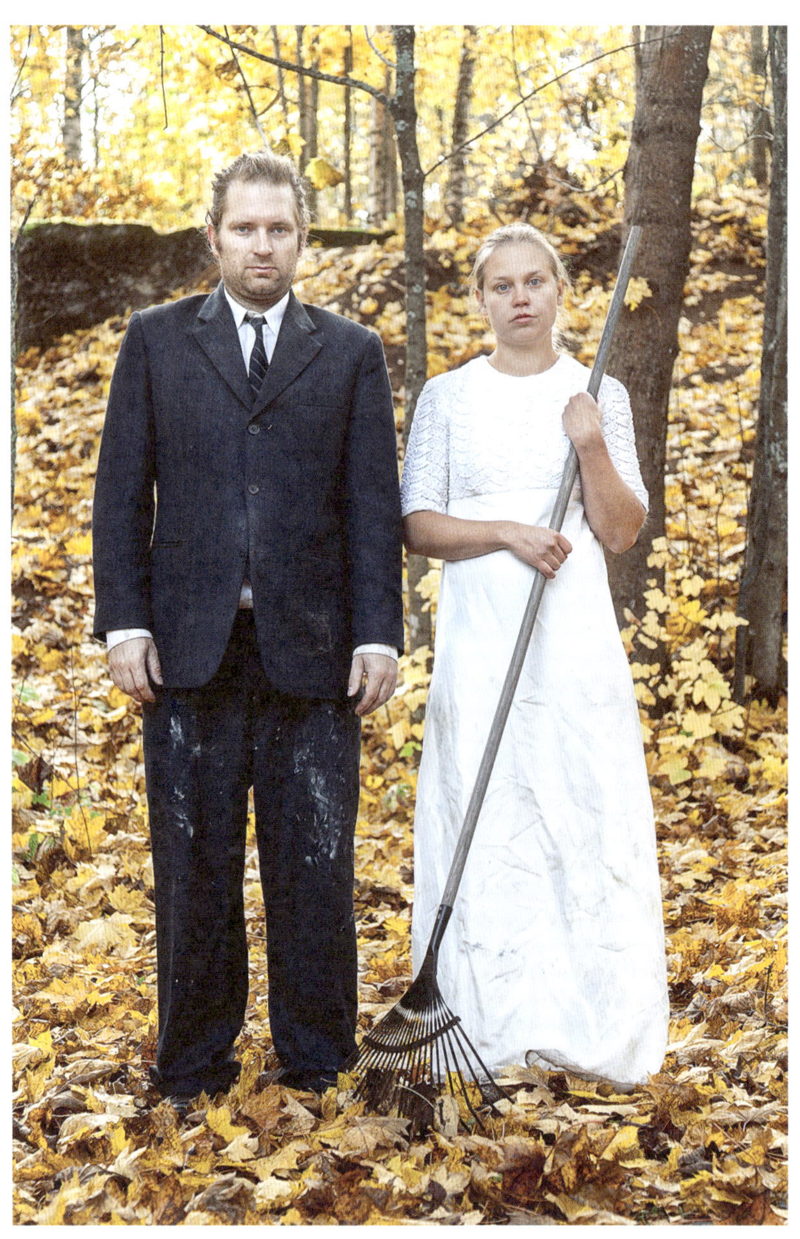

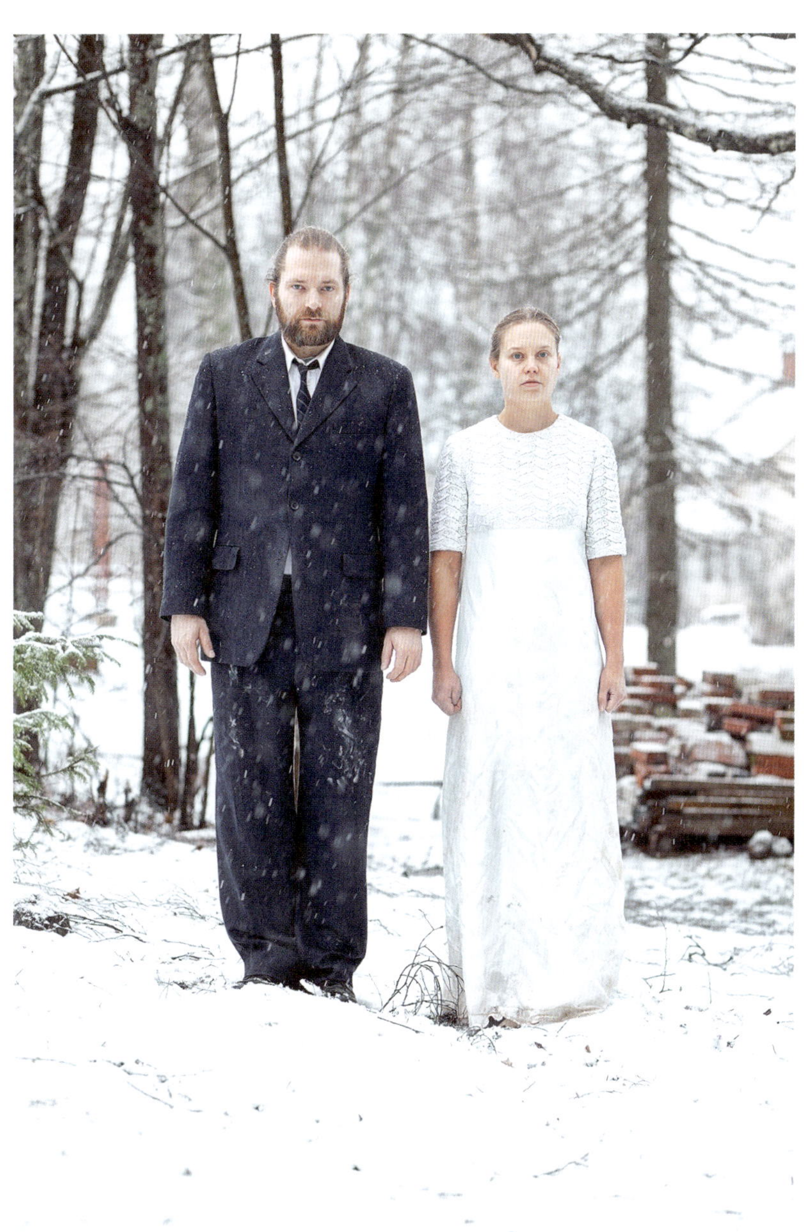

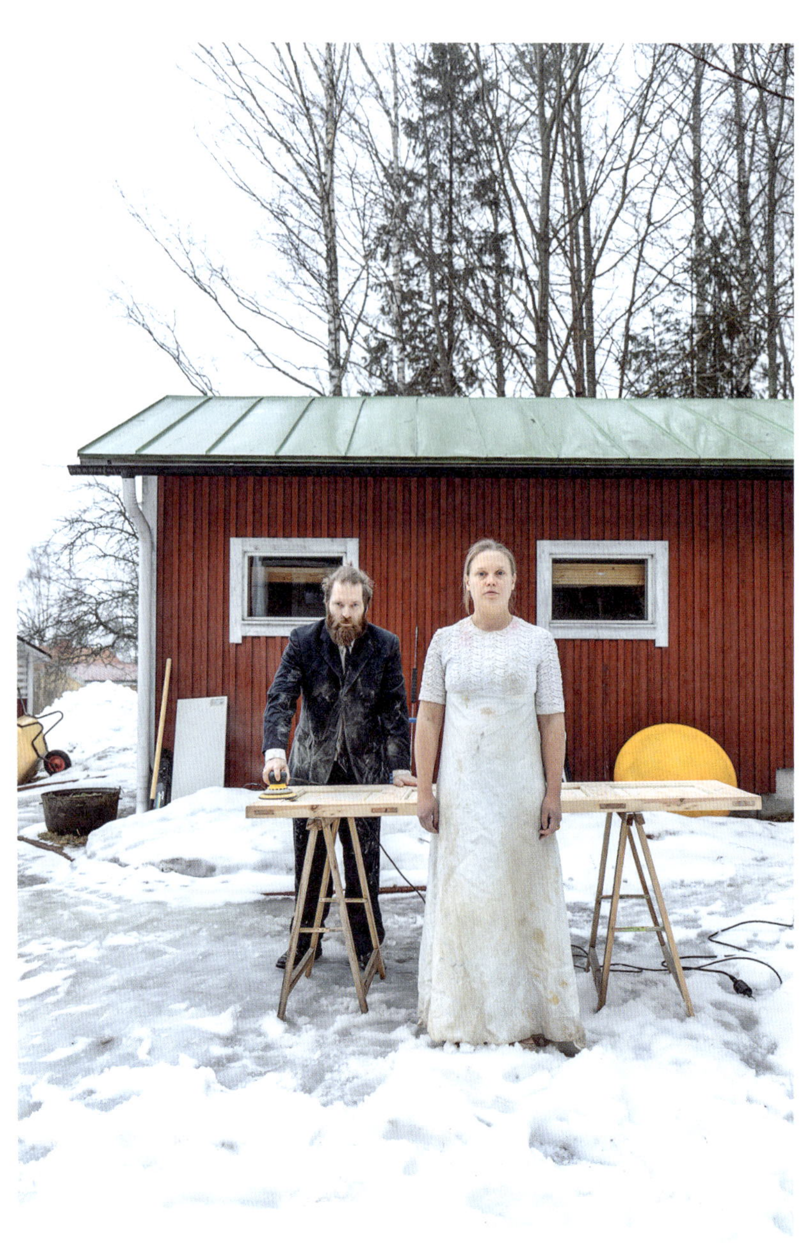

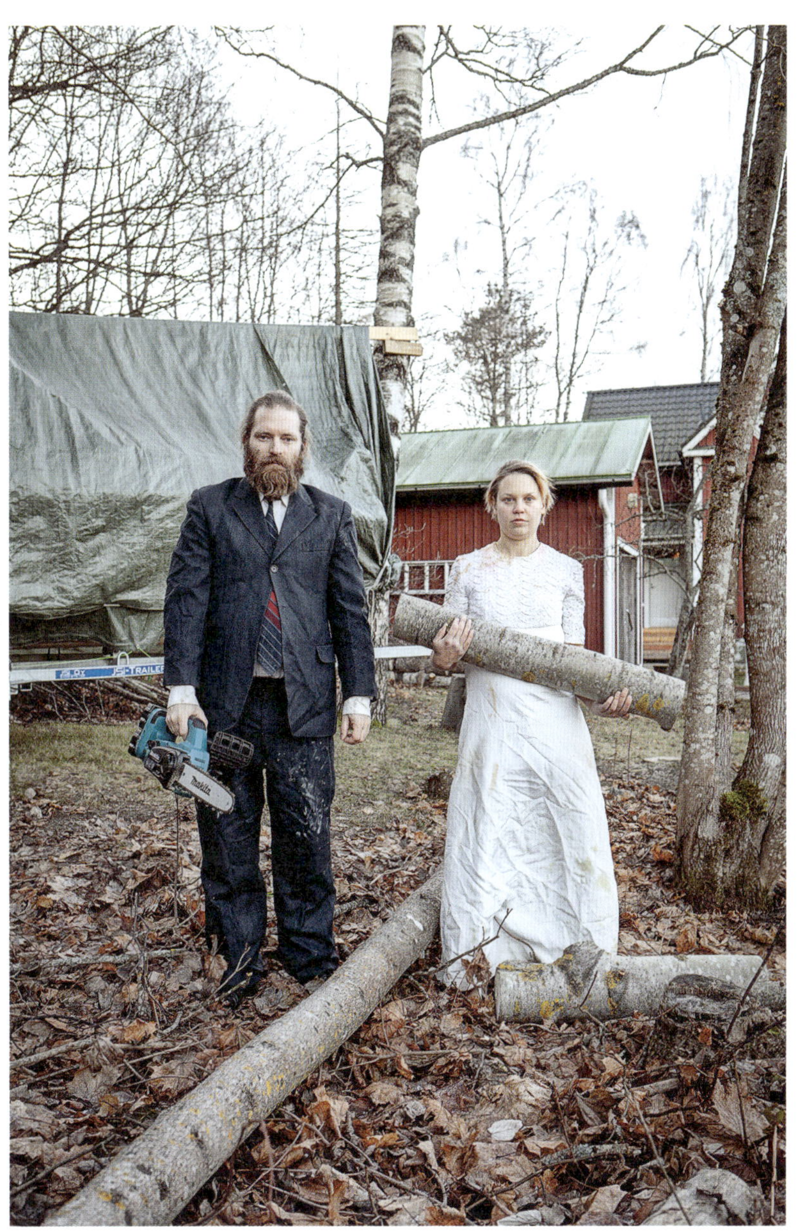

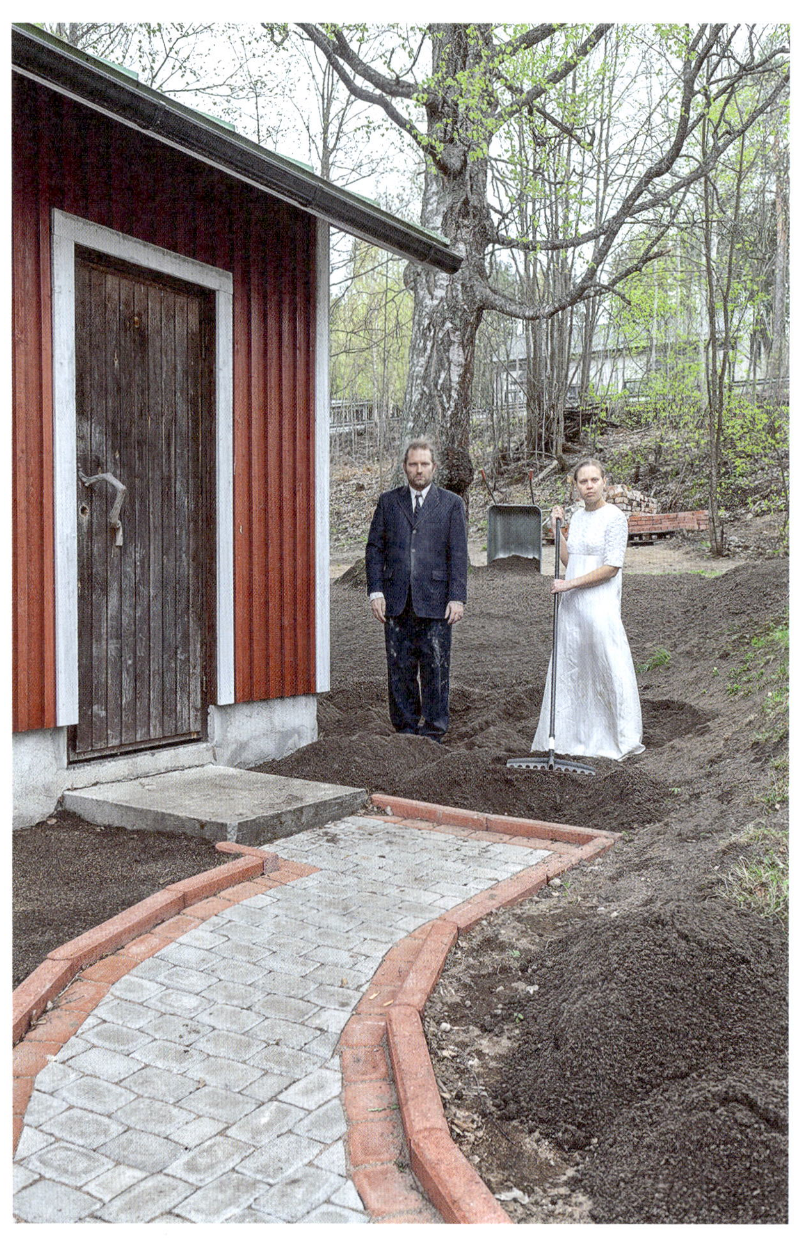

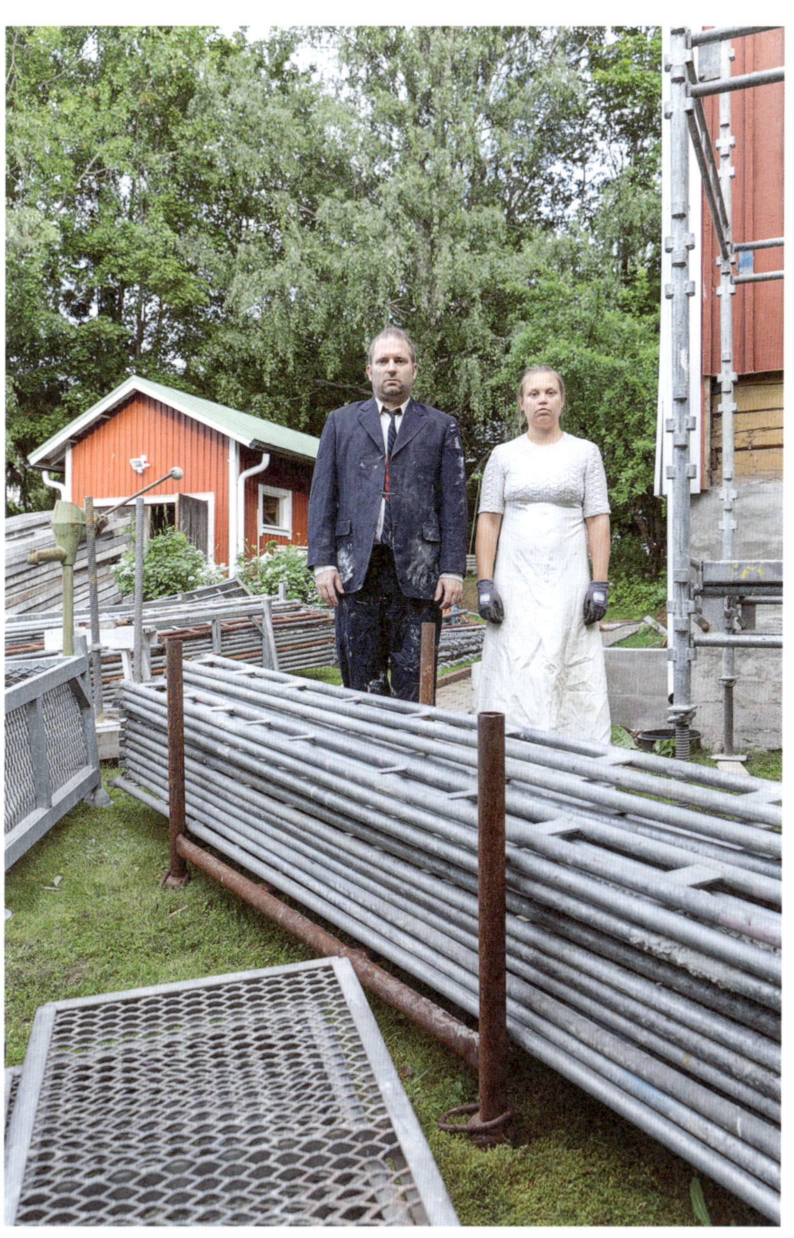

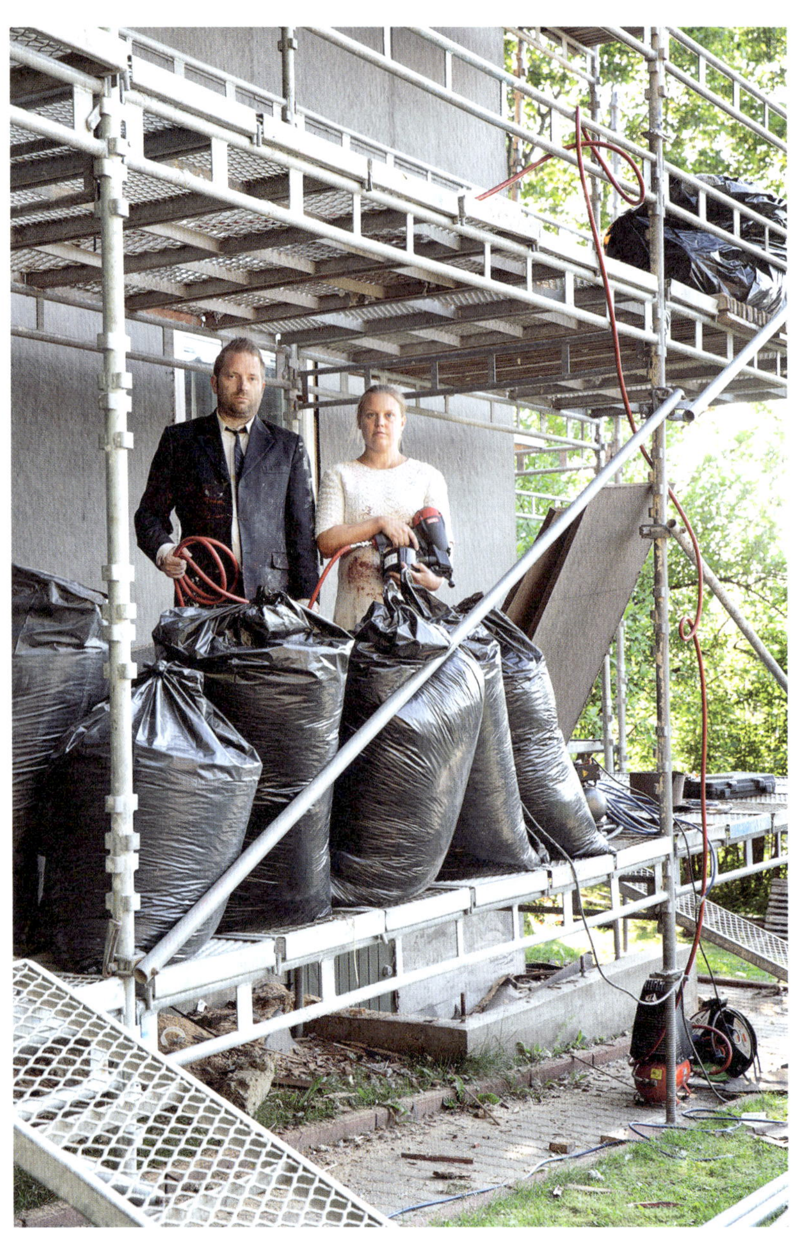

...

Through the years, the cycle of renovation
continued, a perpetual dance of transformation
and frustration. The couple's initial optimism waned,
giving way to moments of doubt and exhaustion.
Yet, their love for the House, like an unyielding
flame, flickered and endured.

...

...

The House, though resistant, could not help but
be moved by the couple's unwavering dedication.
It witnessed their fierce determination and
the way their eyes gleamed with unwavering hope.
Slowly, a subtle shift occurred within its tired
beams. The House began to see itself through
their eyes — not as a burden, but as a canvas for
endless possibility.

...

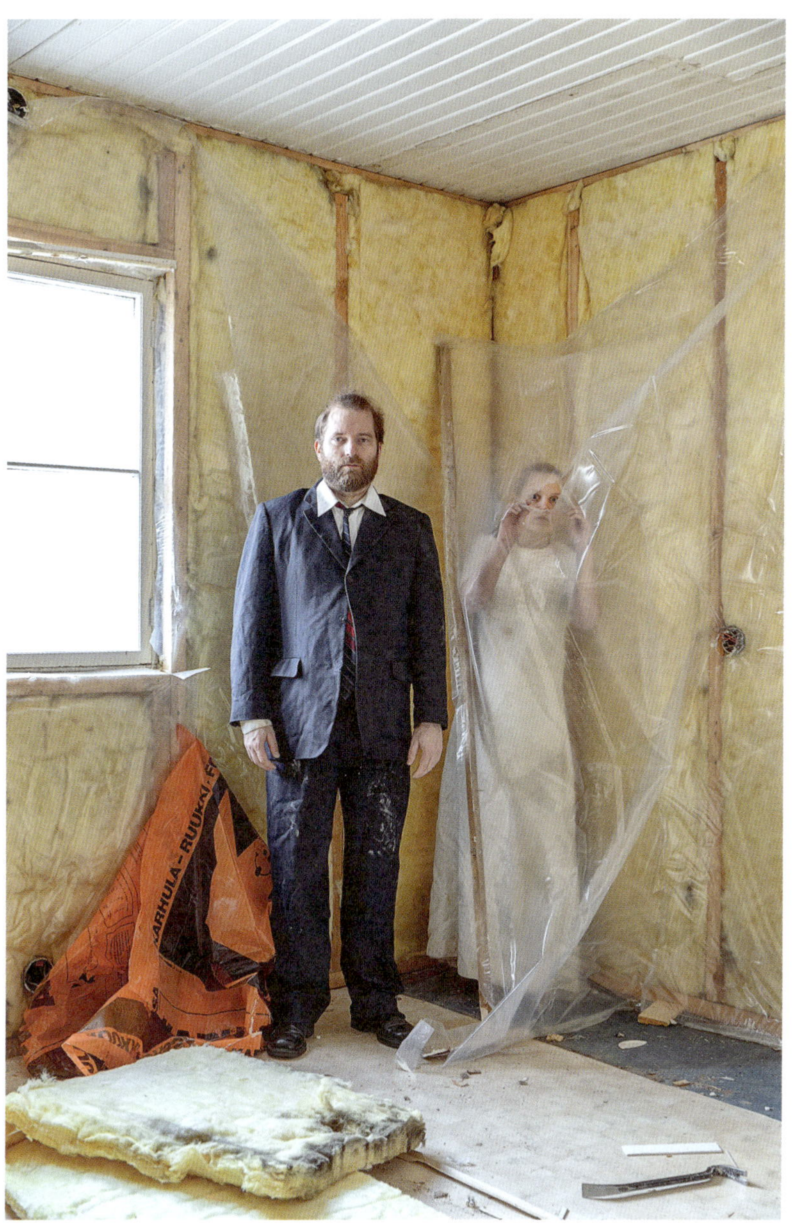

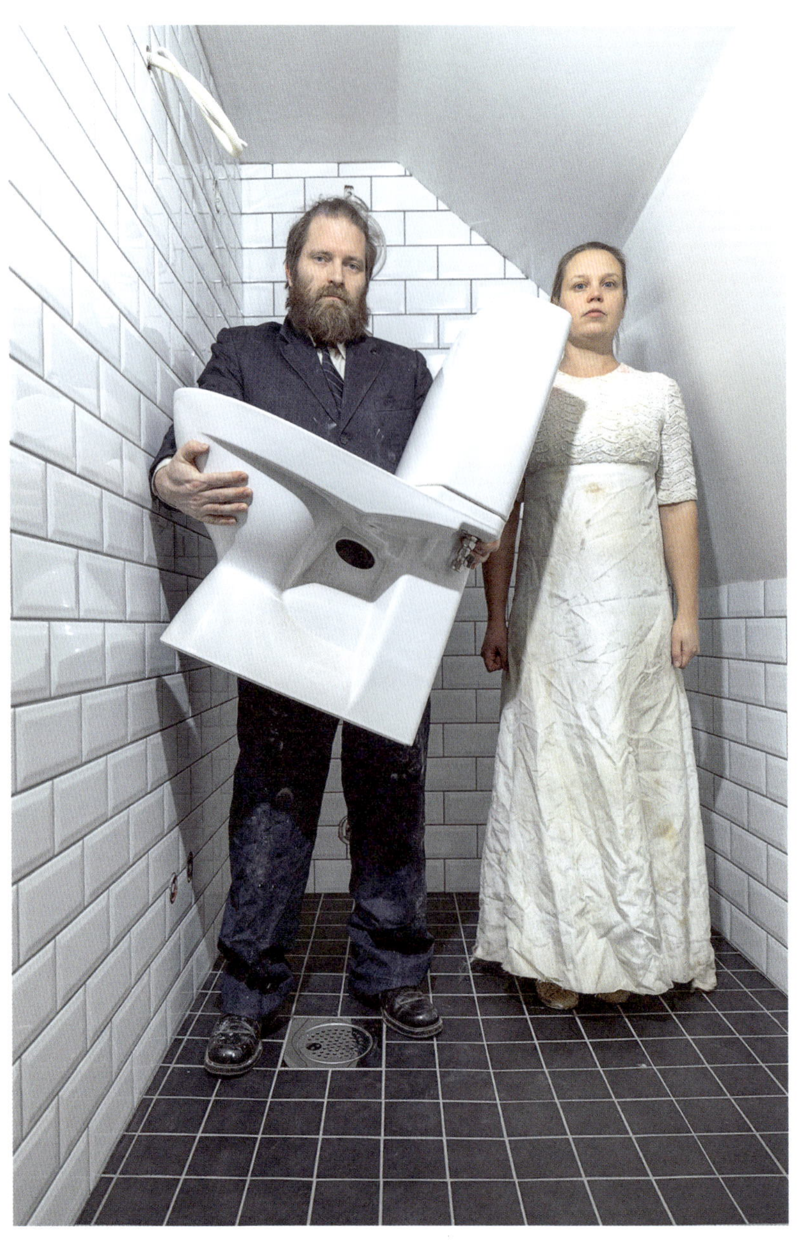

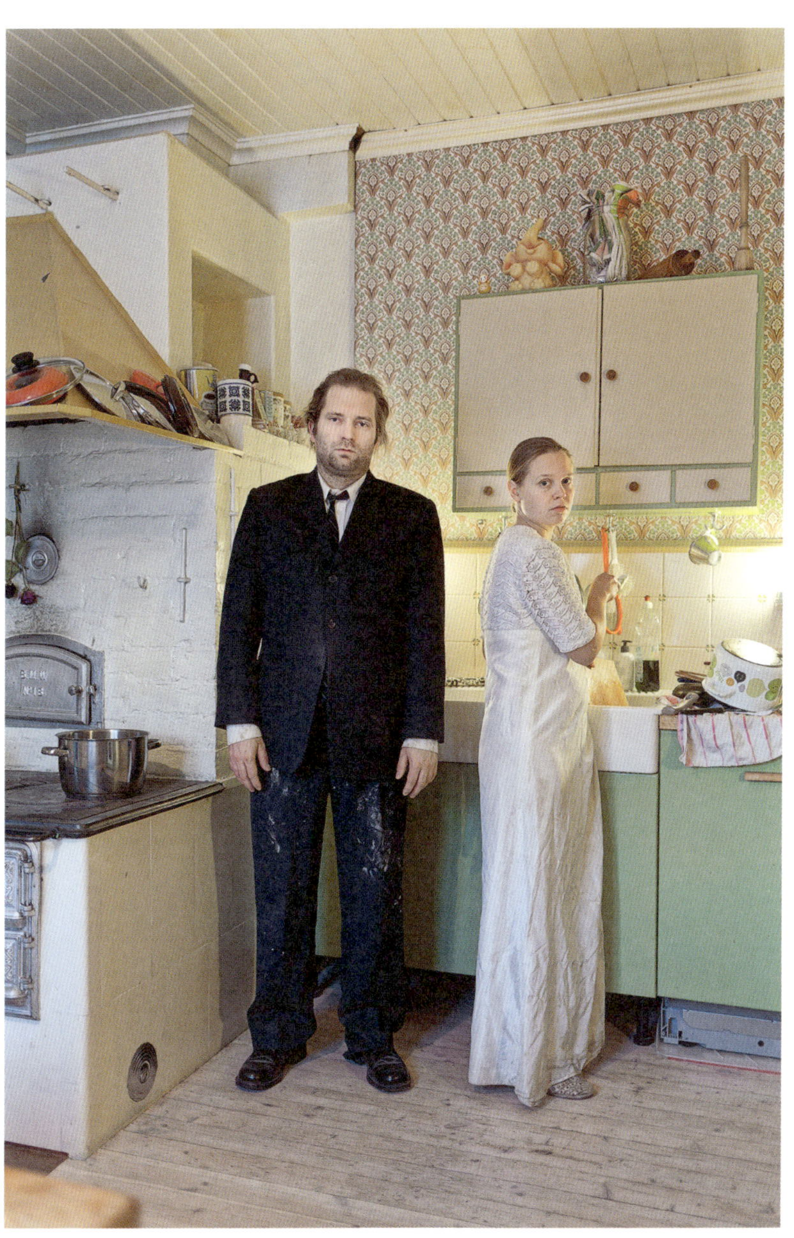

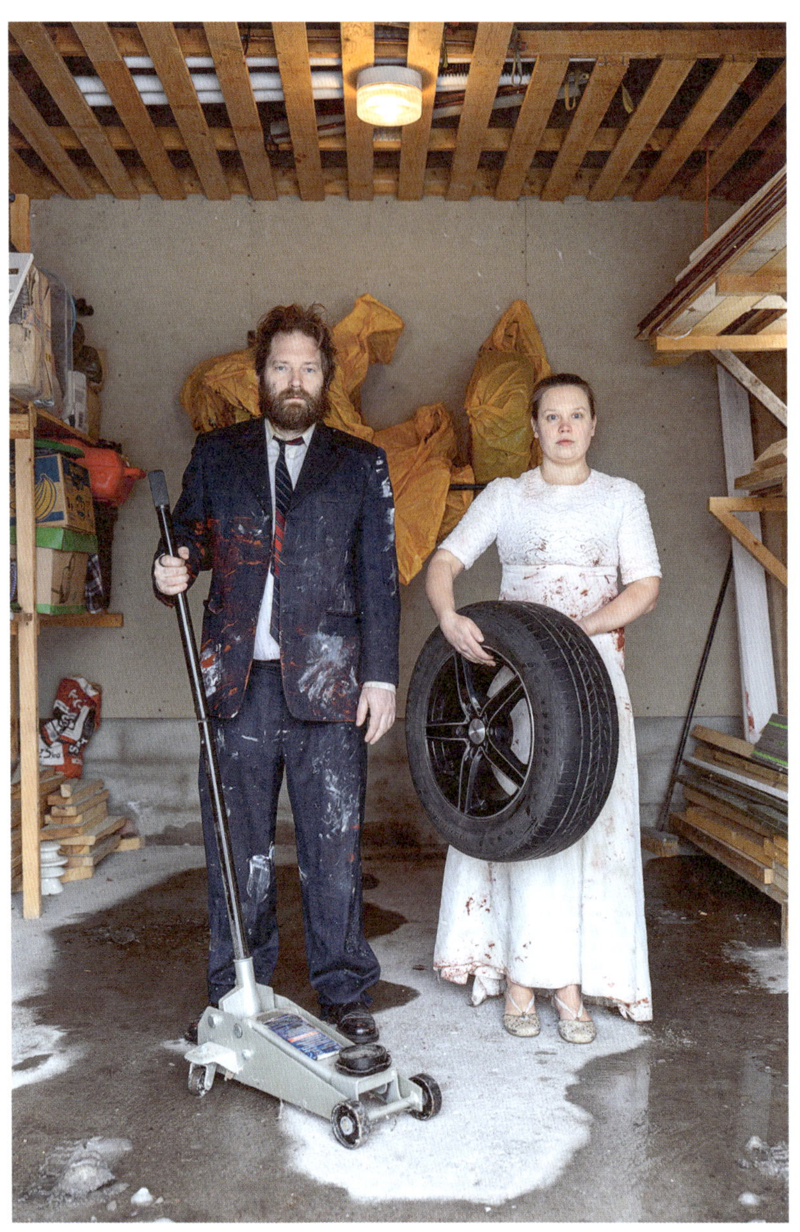

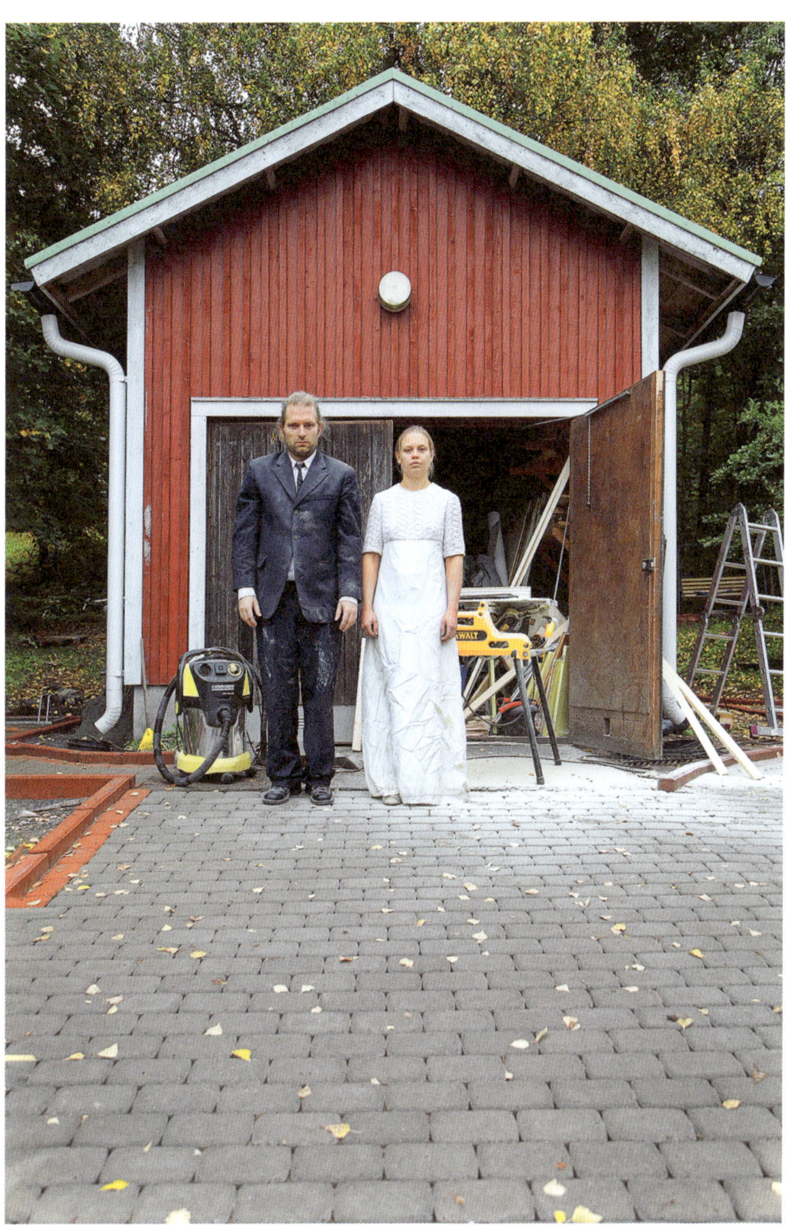

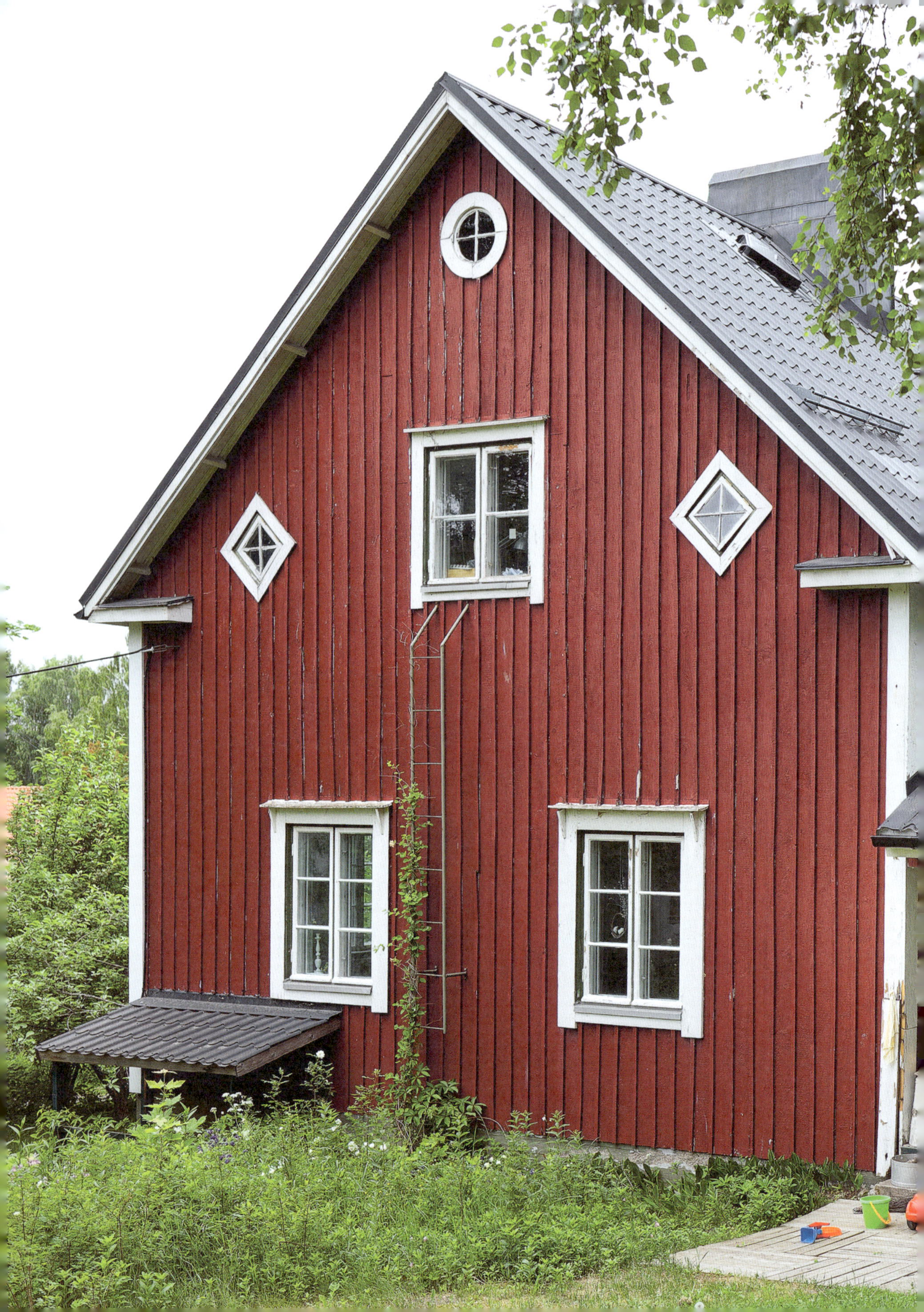

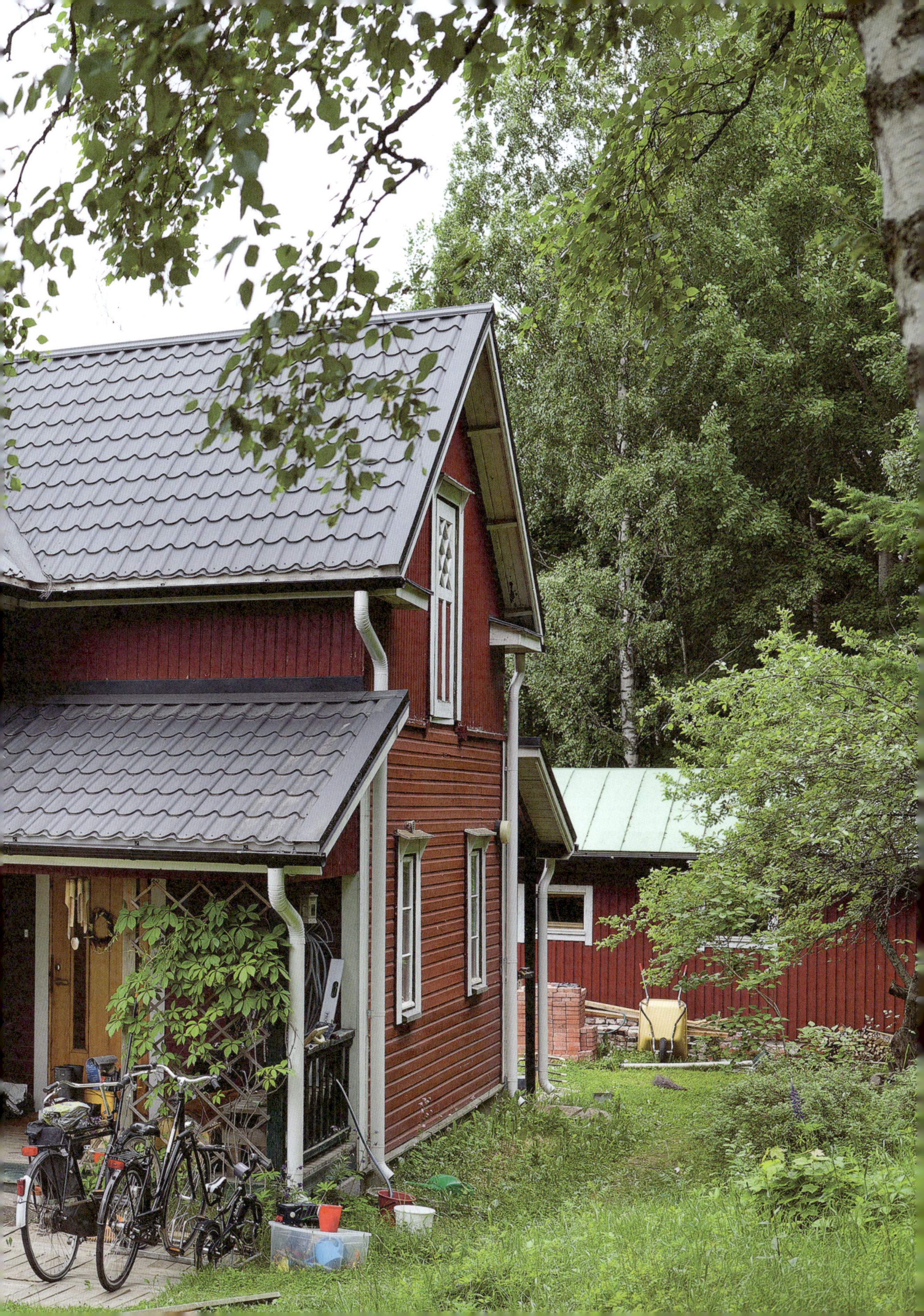

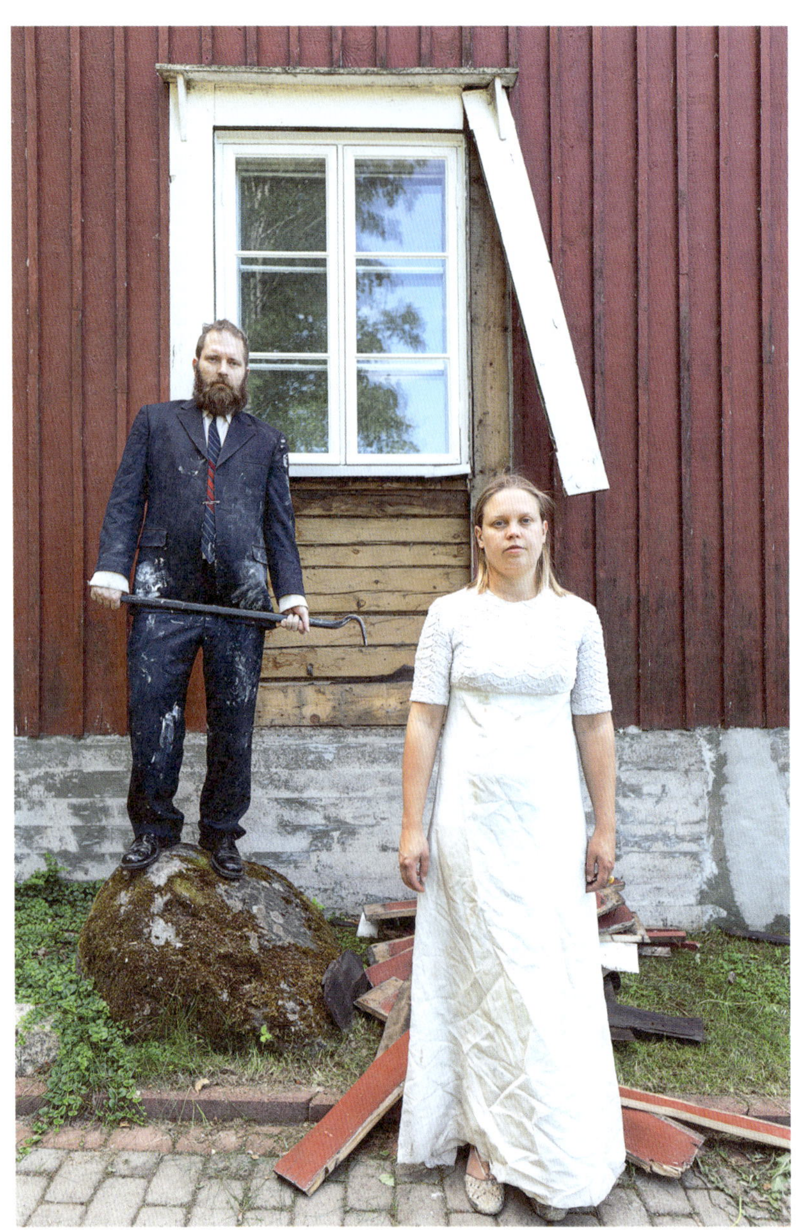

...

With each passing project, the House and the couple
grew together. They learned the art of compromise,
navigating the labyrinth of renovation with a blend
of patience and resilience. They faced setbacks
and challenges, yet they refused to succumb to
the notion of defeat. Instead, they embraced
the never-ending nature of the work, finding
solace in the shared journey of growth.

...

...

And so, the House's renovation became
a perpetual symphony, the sounds of hammers
and drills harmonizing with the couple's laughter
and occasional frustration. It became a testament
to their enduring love, a testament to the beauty
that arises from embracing the ongoing process
of transformation.

...

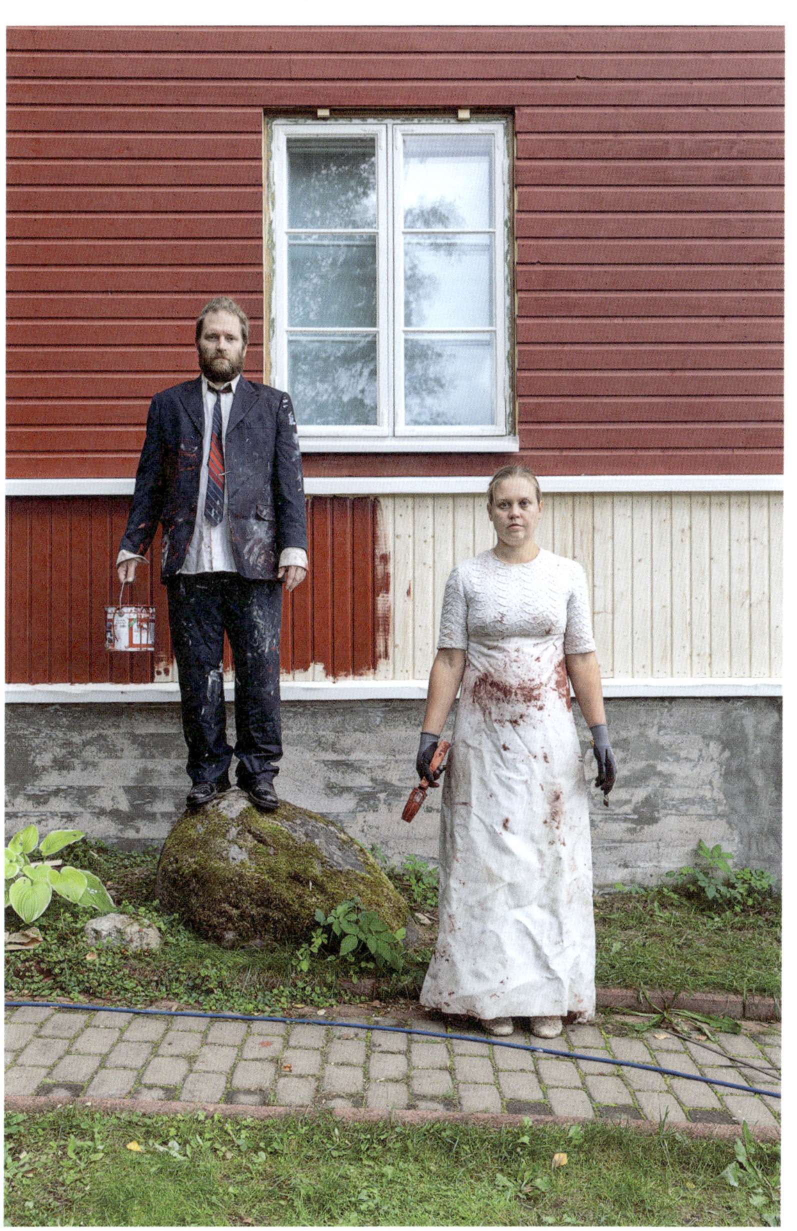

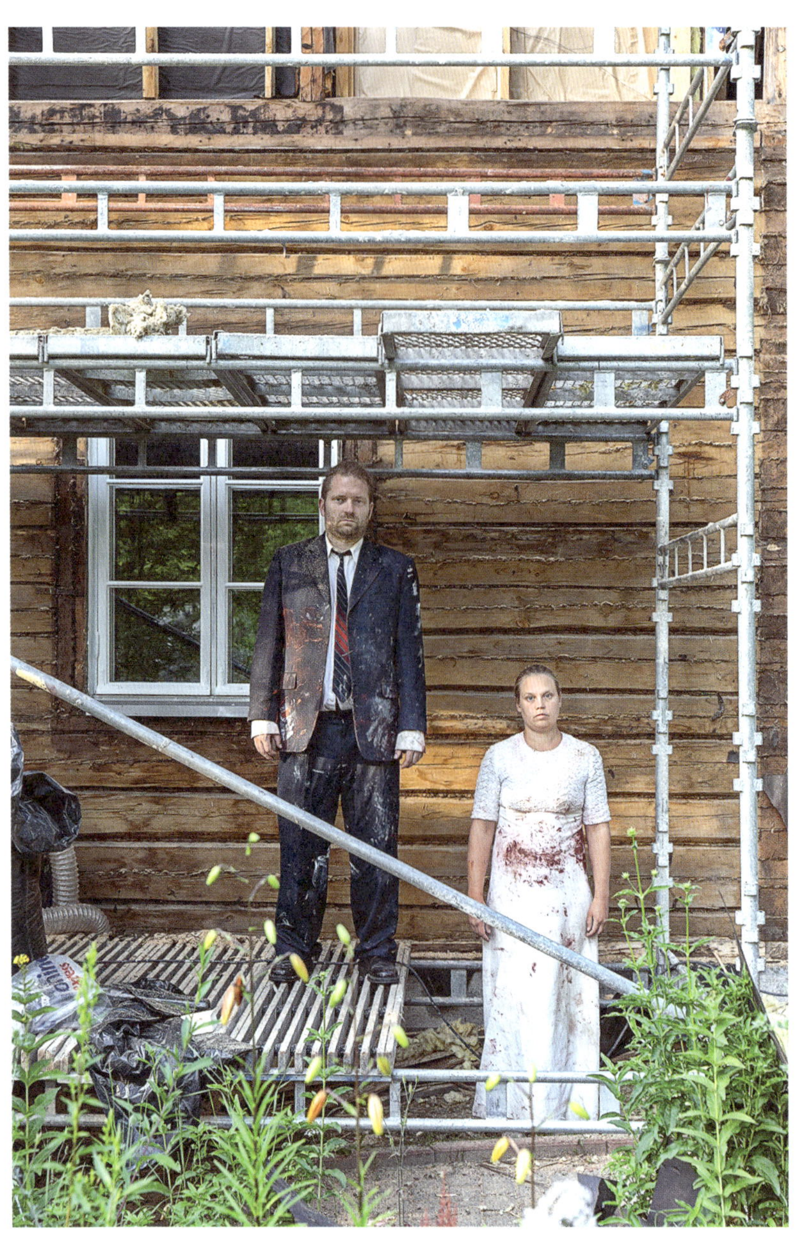

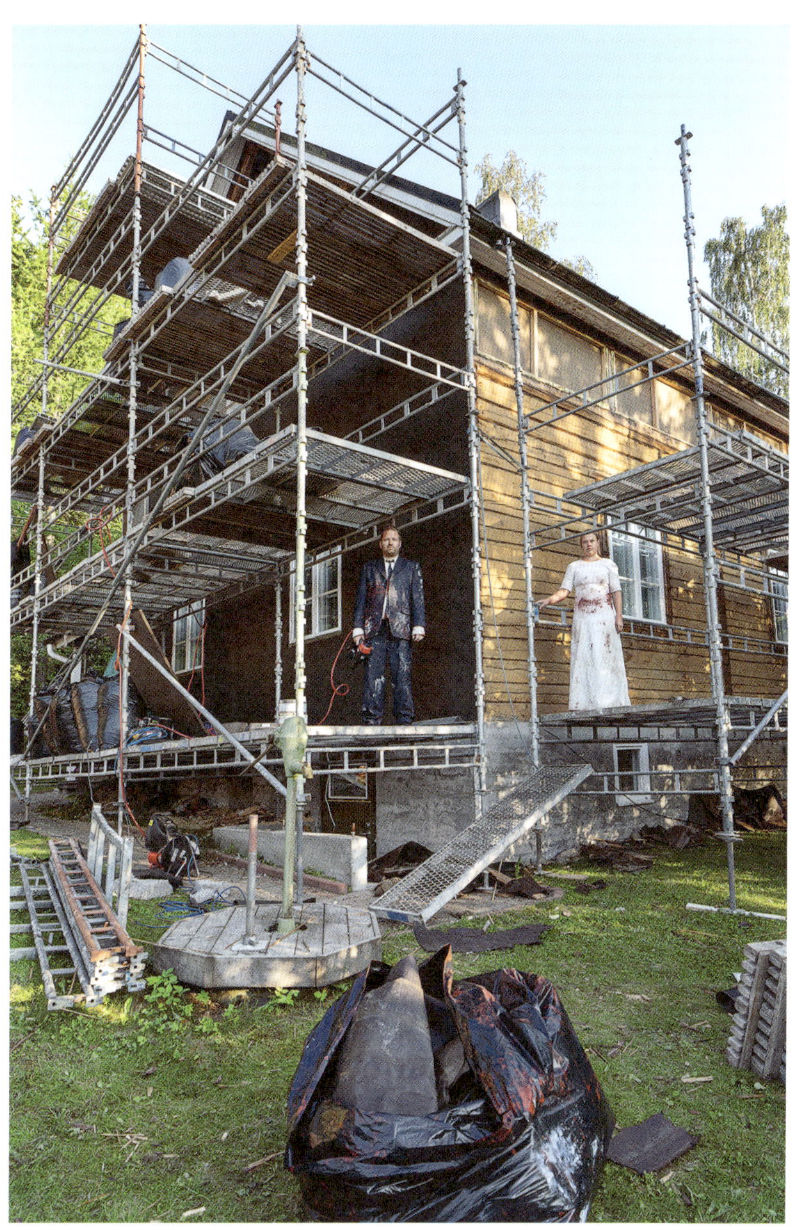

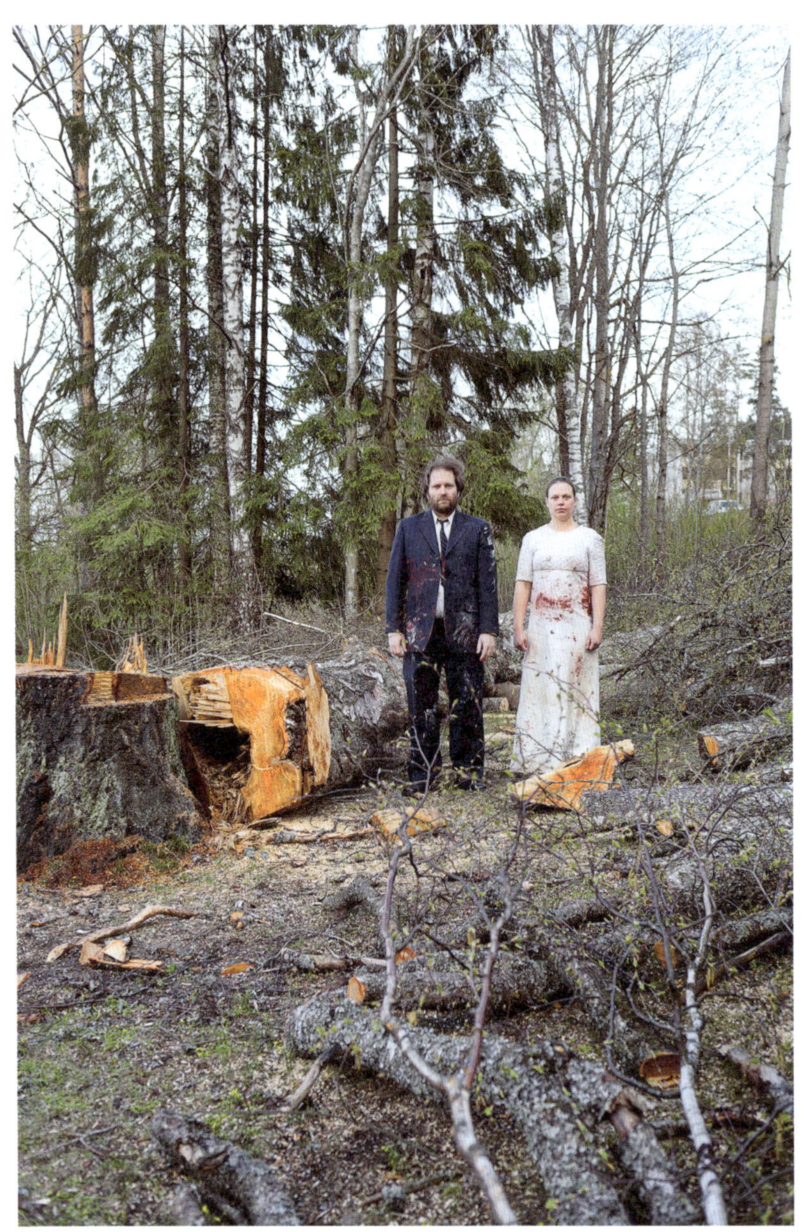

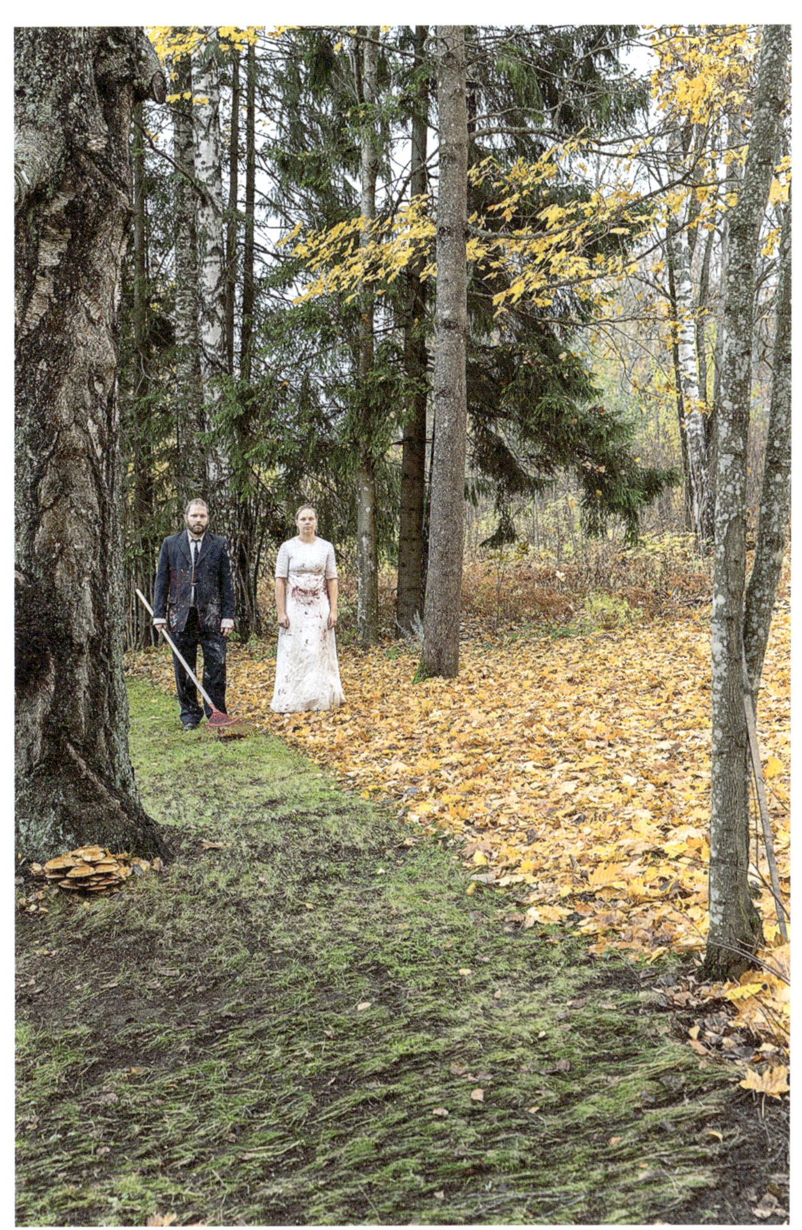

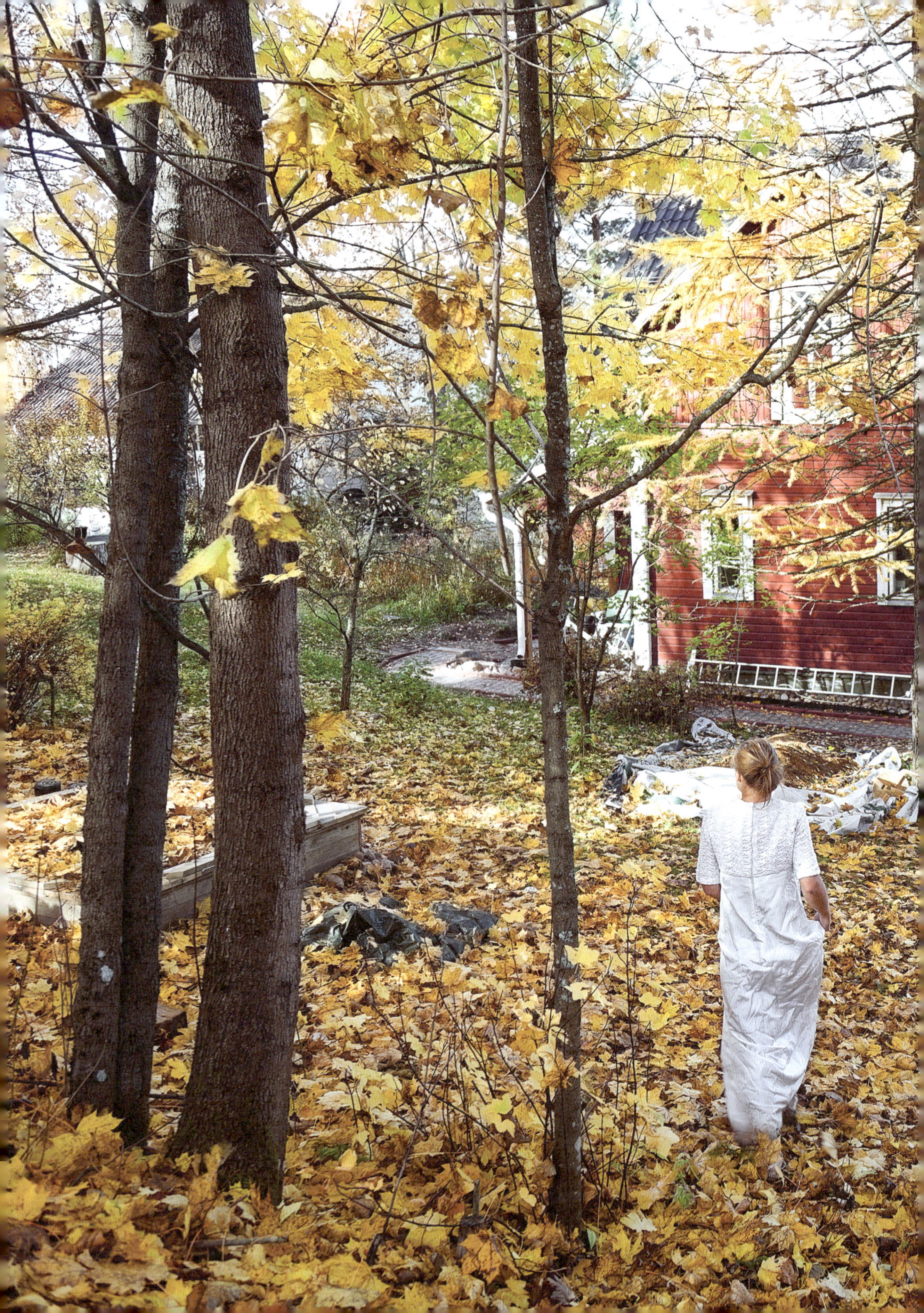

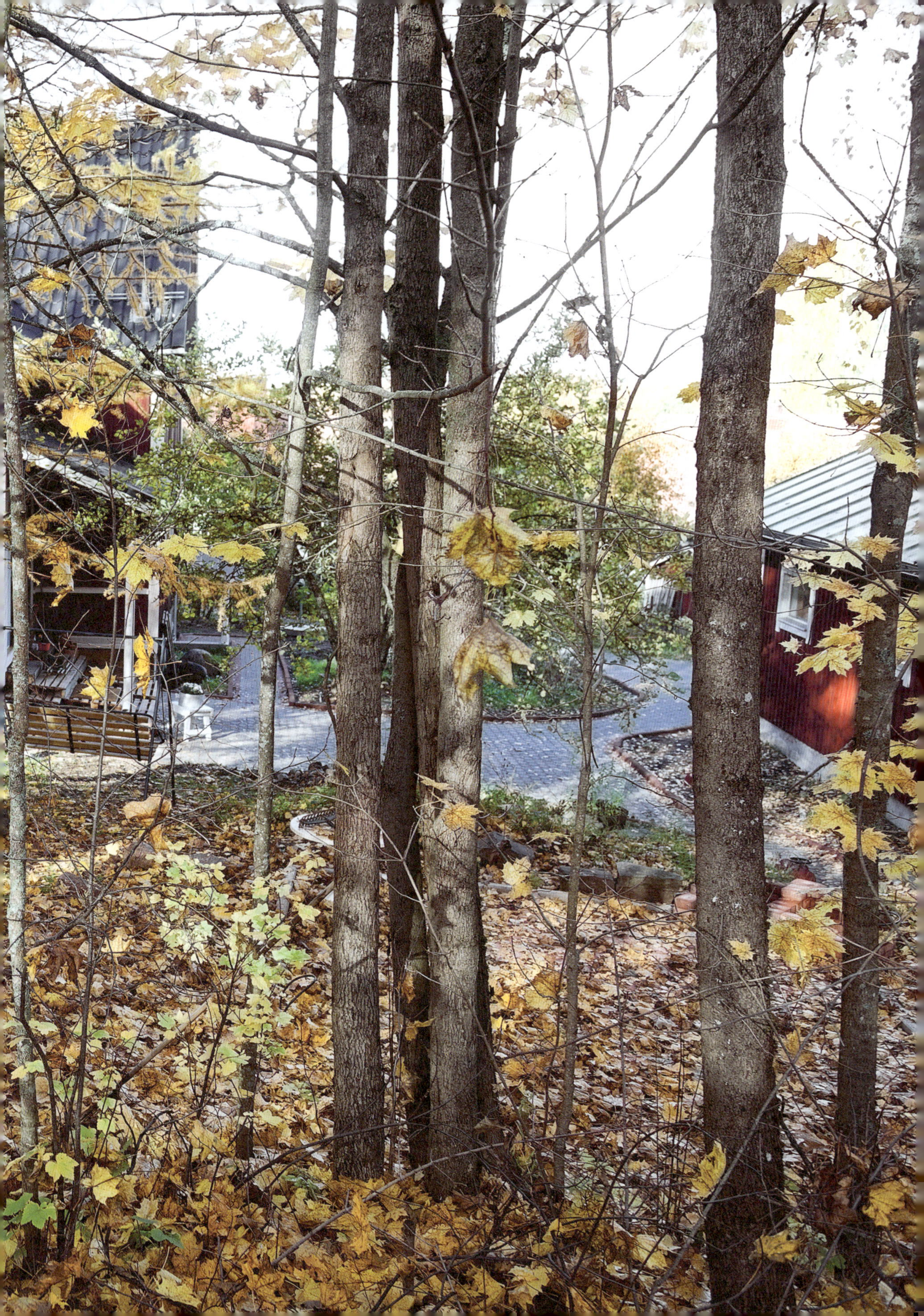

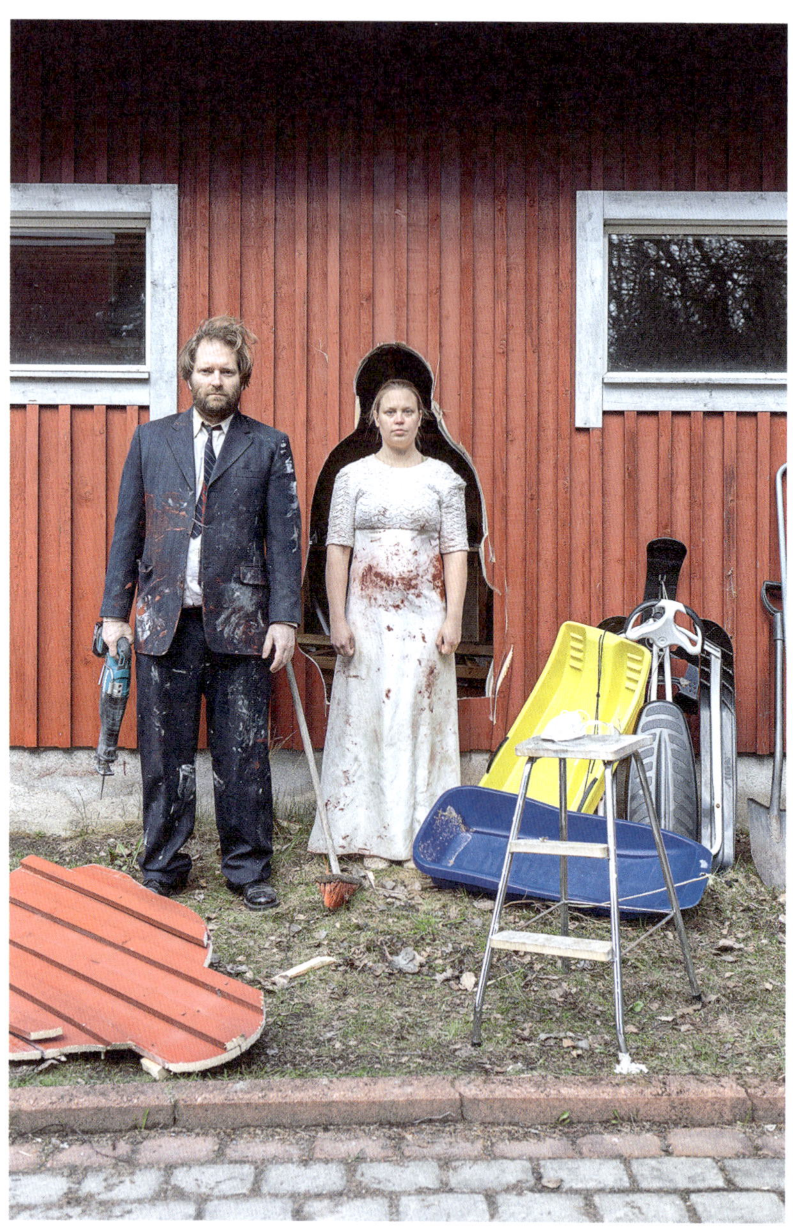

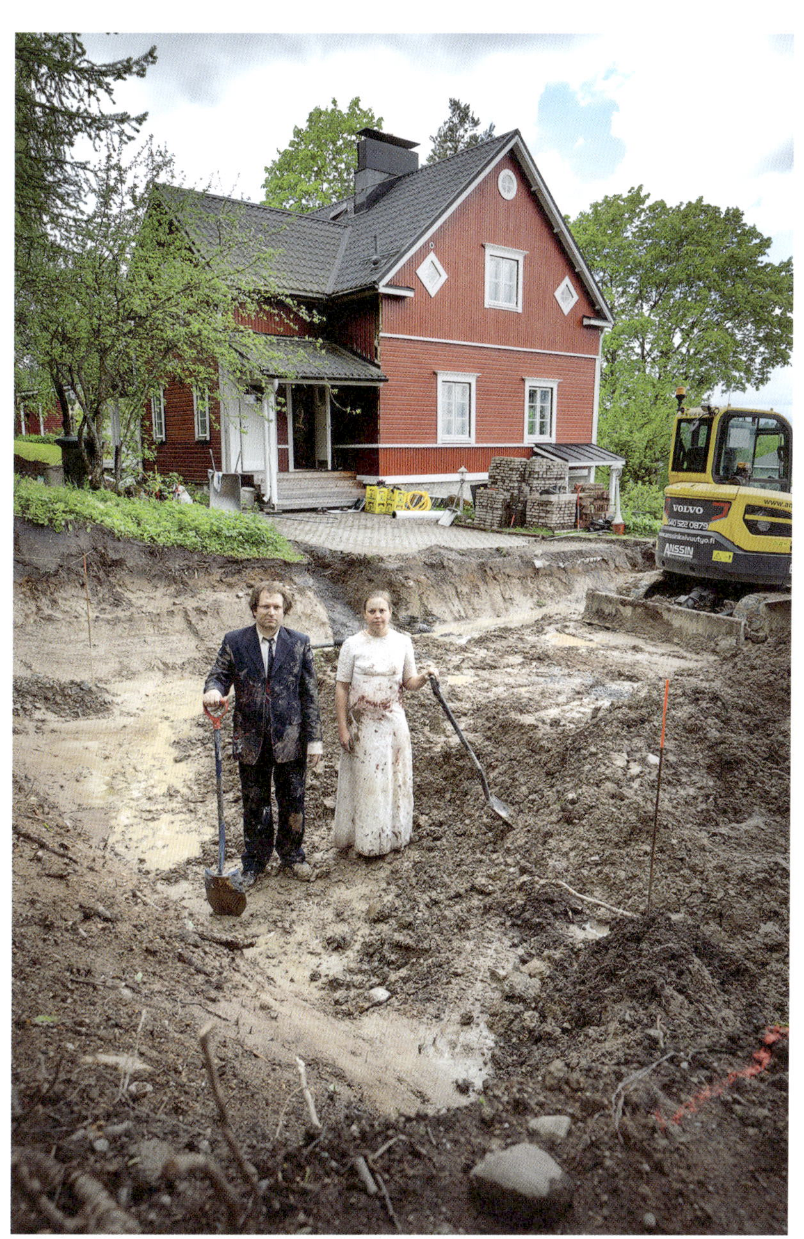

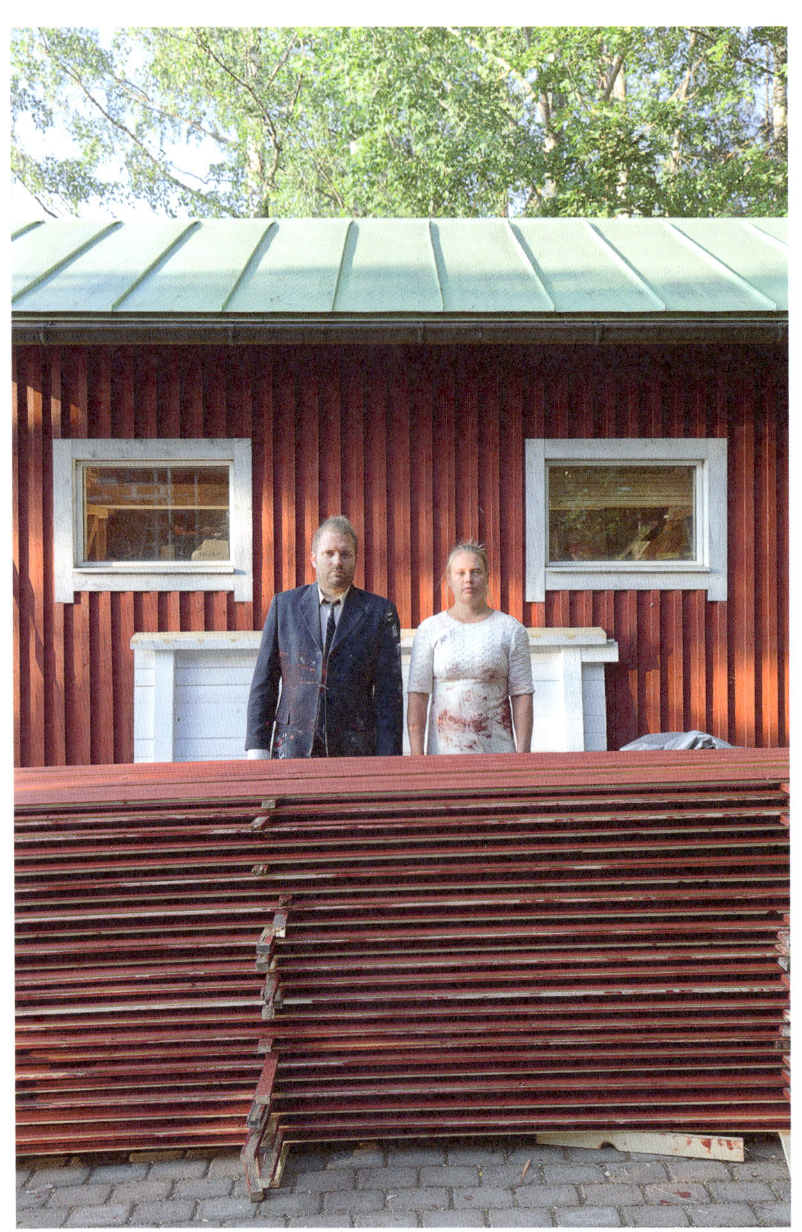

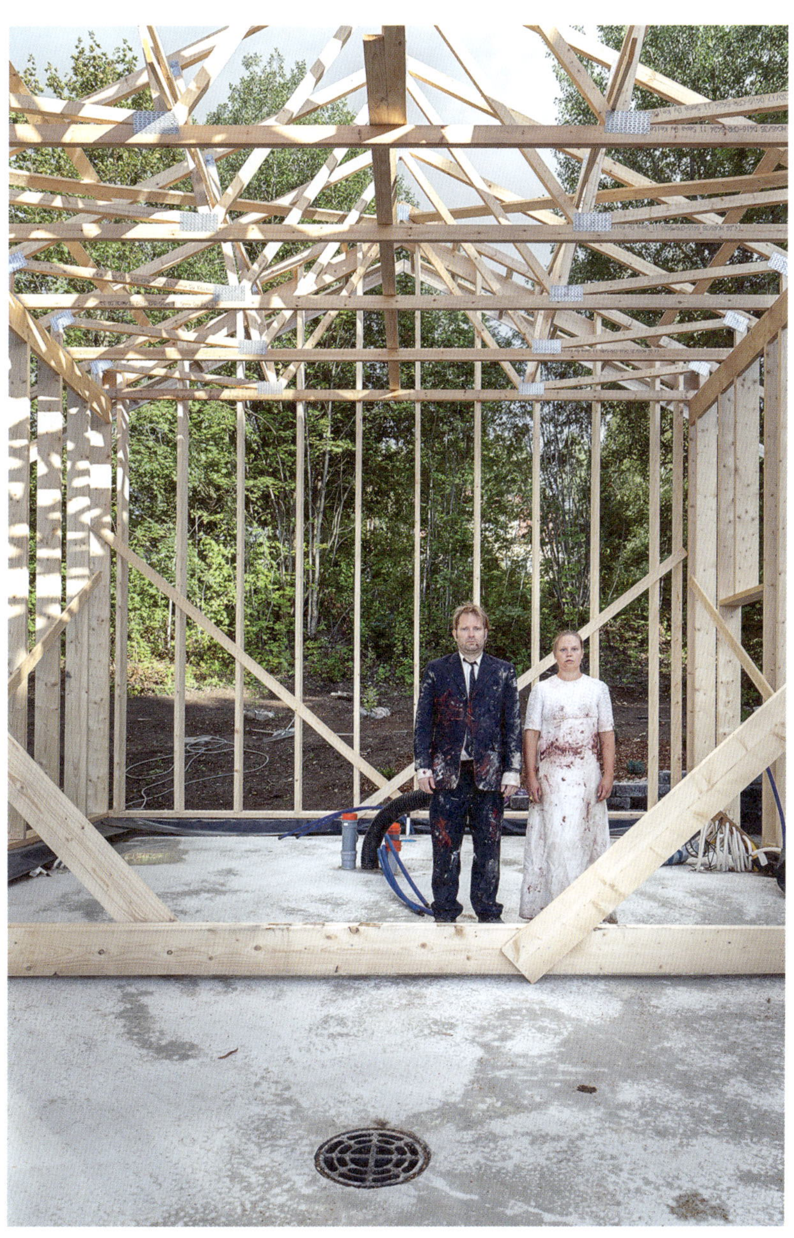

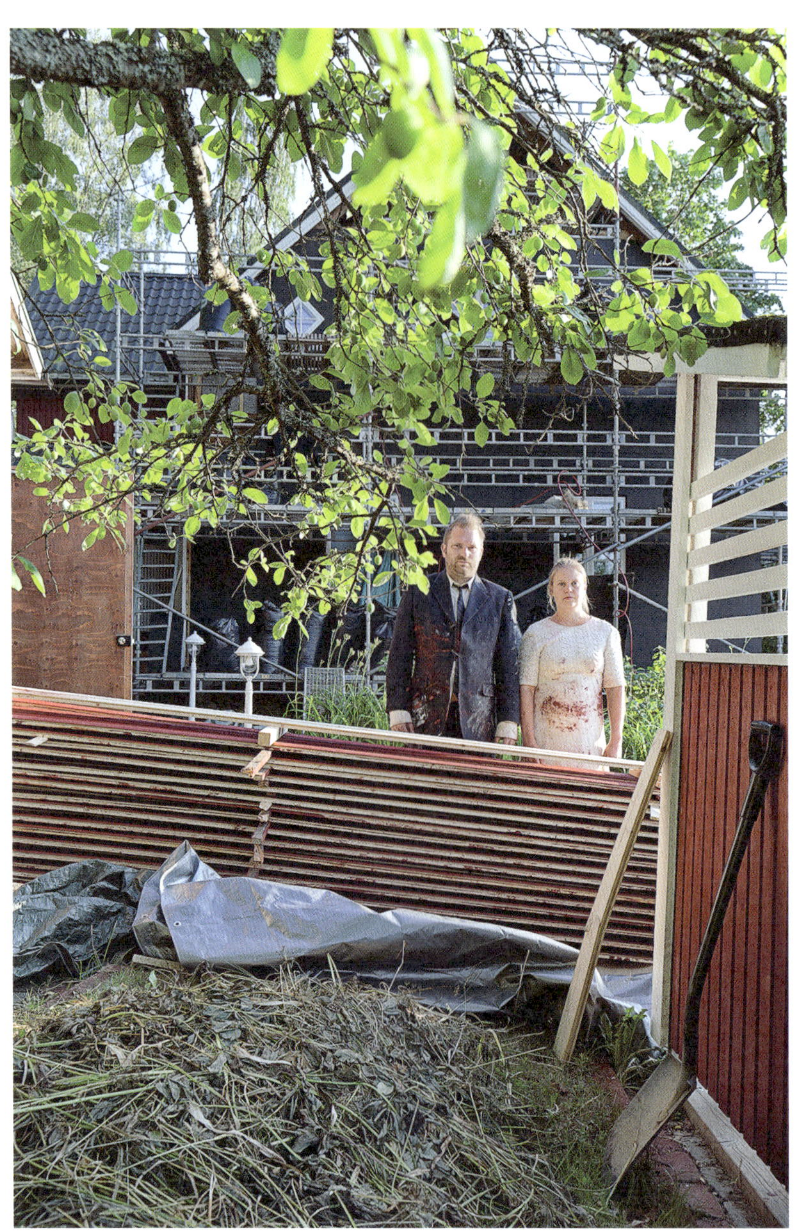

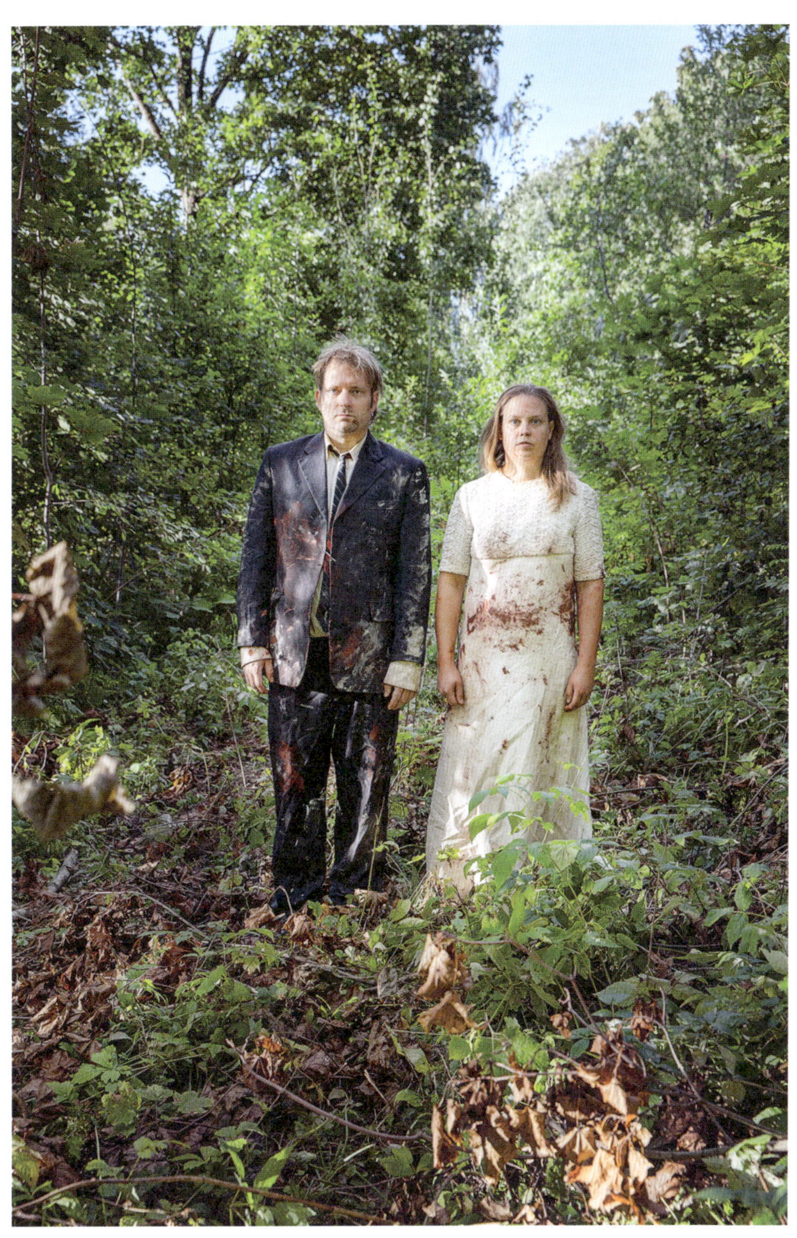

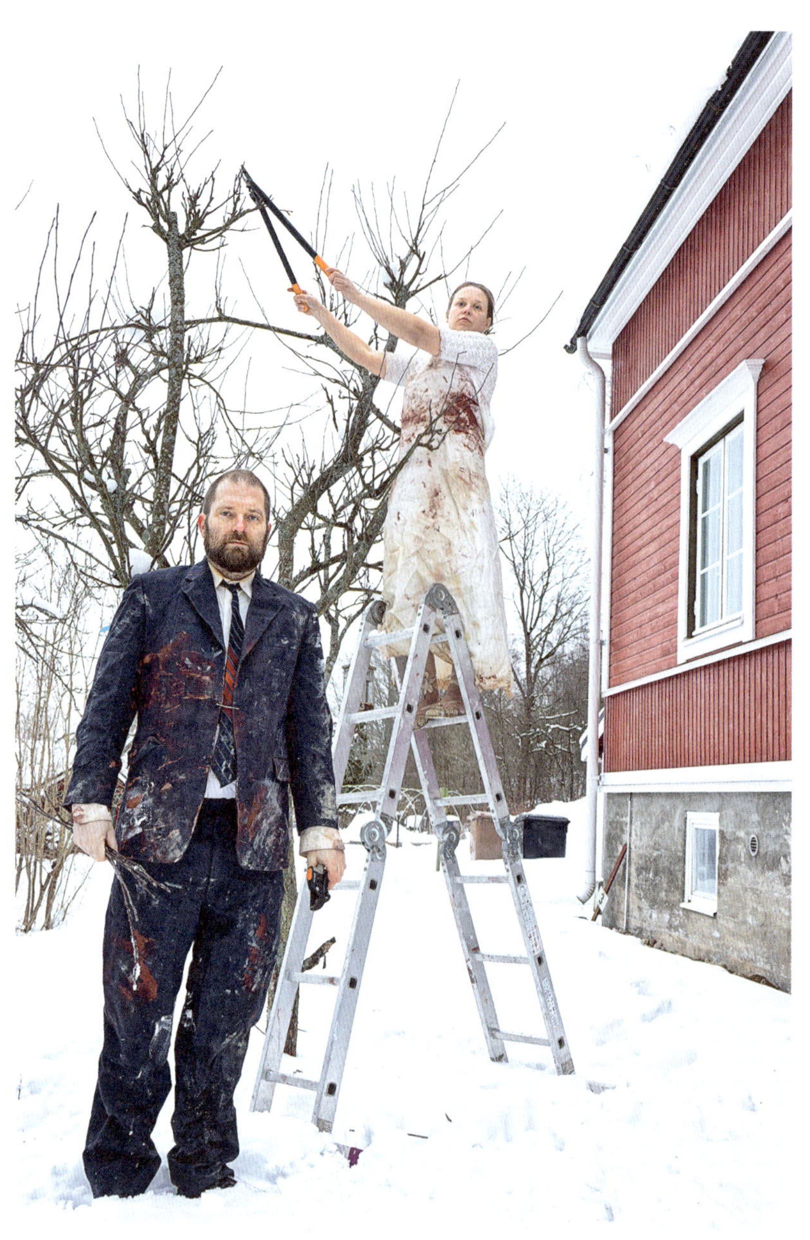

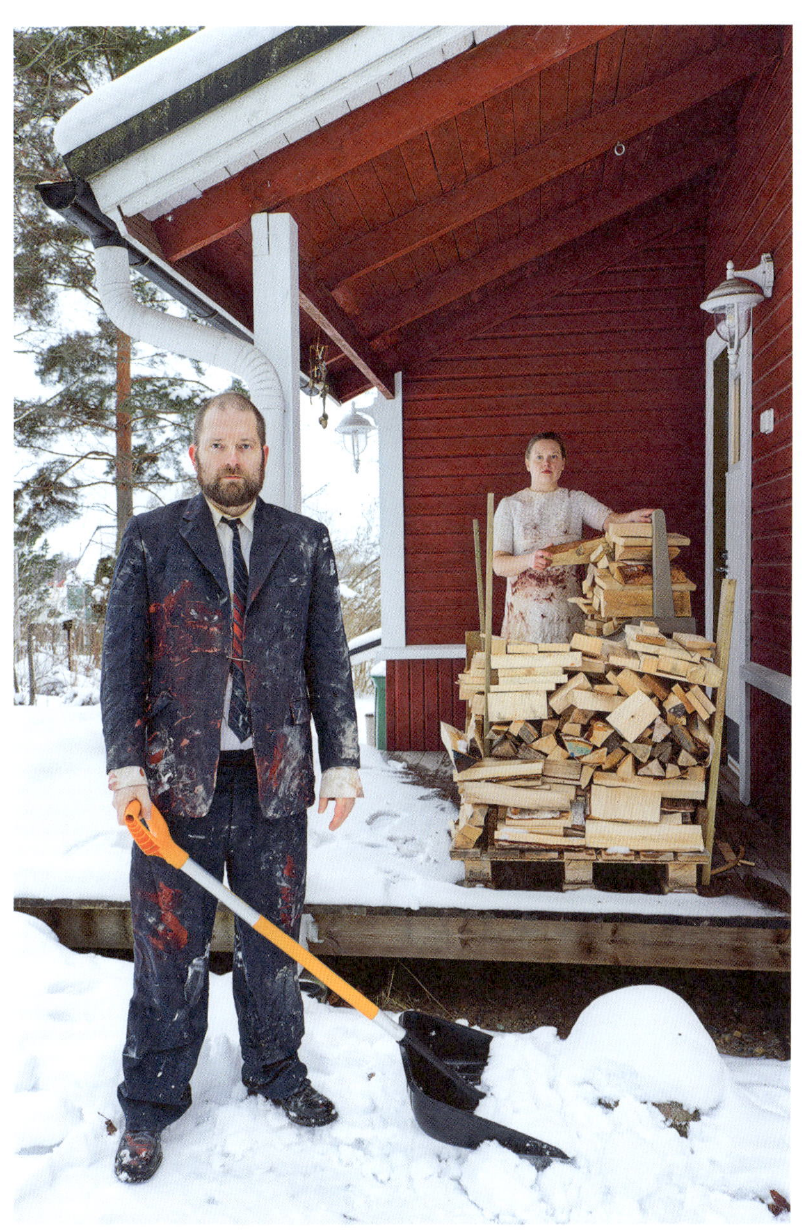

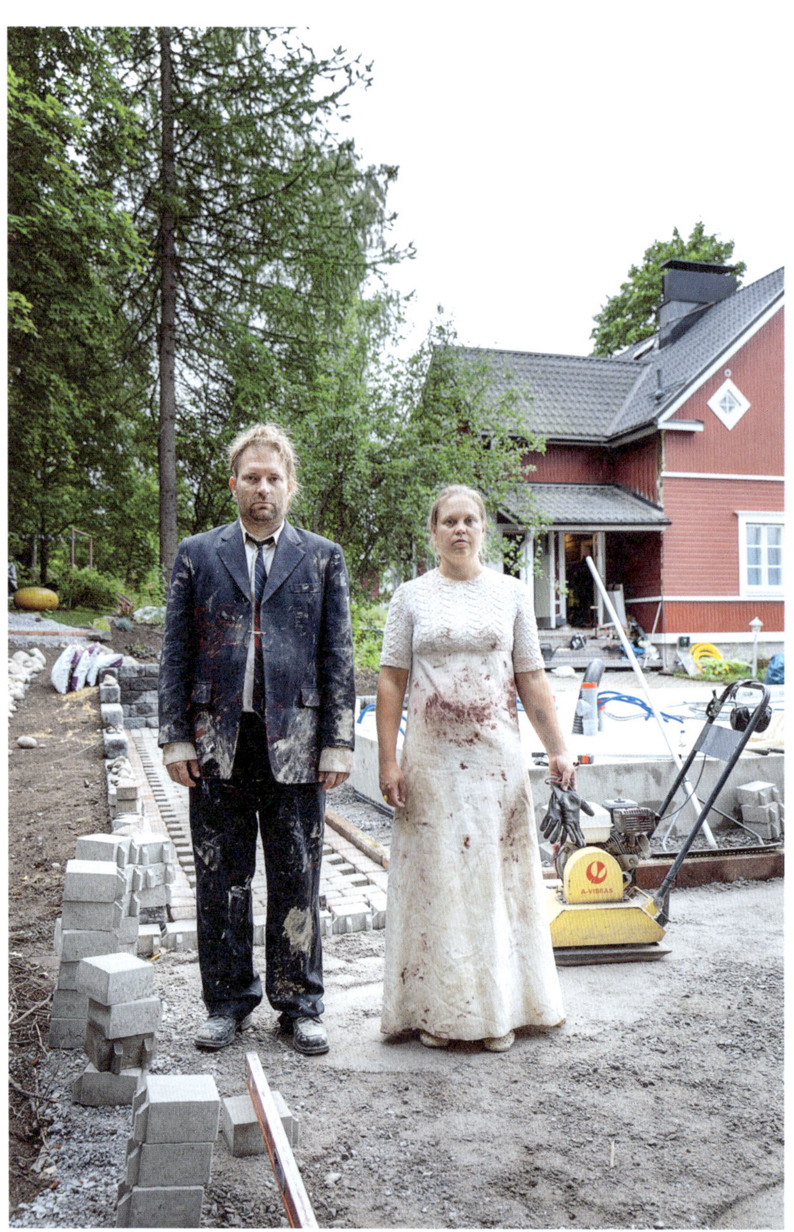

...

The House, once grumpy and resistant,
now bore witness to the couple's unwavering
devotion. It had become a home where stories
intermingled with layers of fresh paint, where
the echoes of hard work and perseverance resided.
The couple had discovered that true renovation
is not merely about fixing the physical aspects
of a House, but also about the continual renewal
of their connection, their shared resilience.

...

...

And so, the cycle of renovation persisted, its rhythm
becoming a familiar heartbeat in the House's core.
The couple and the House, bound together in
an eternal dance, found solace in the never-ending
journey. For in the midst of endless projects
and weariness, they discovered that the true
beauty lies not in reaching a destination but in
the transformative power of the ongoing process.

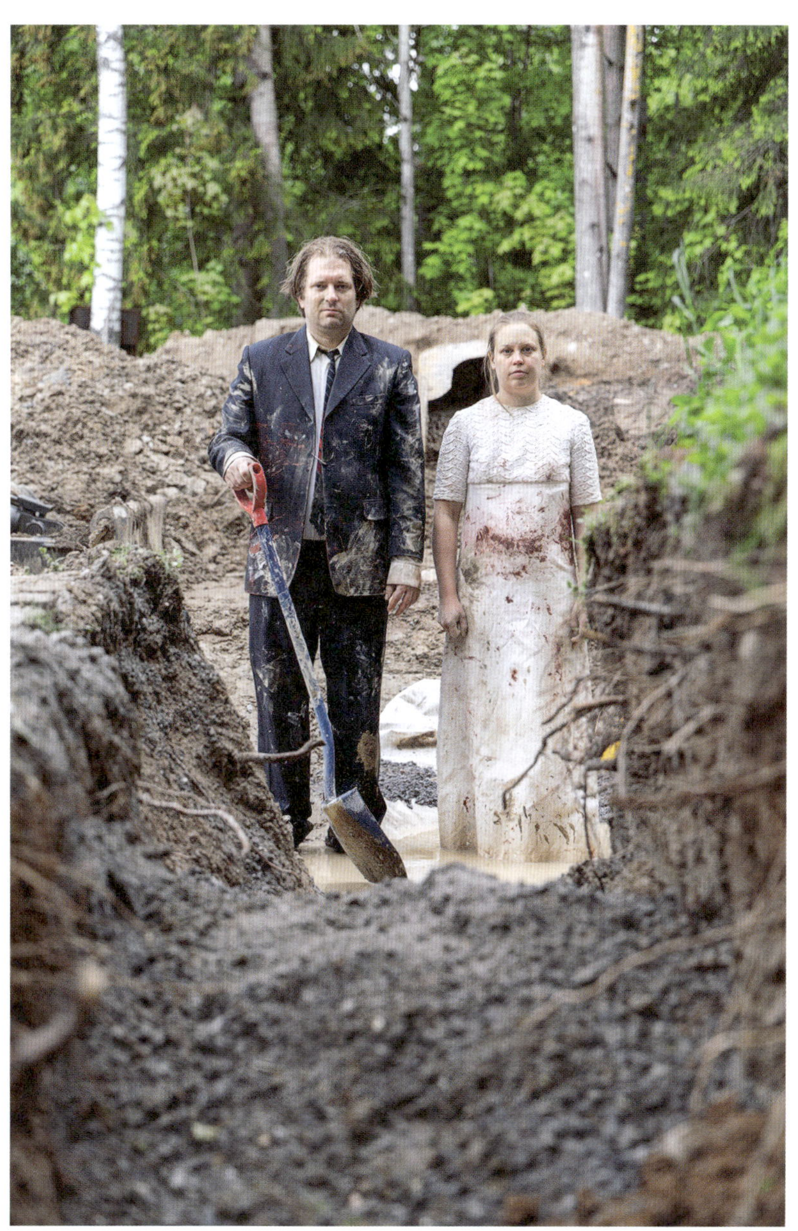

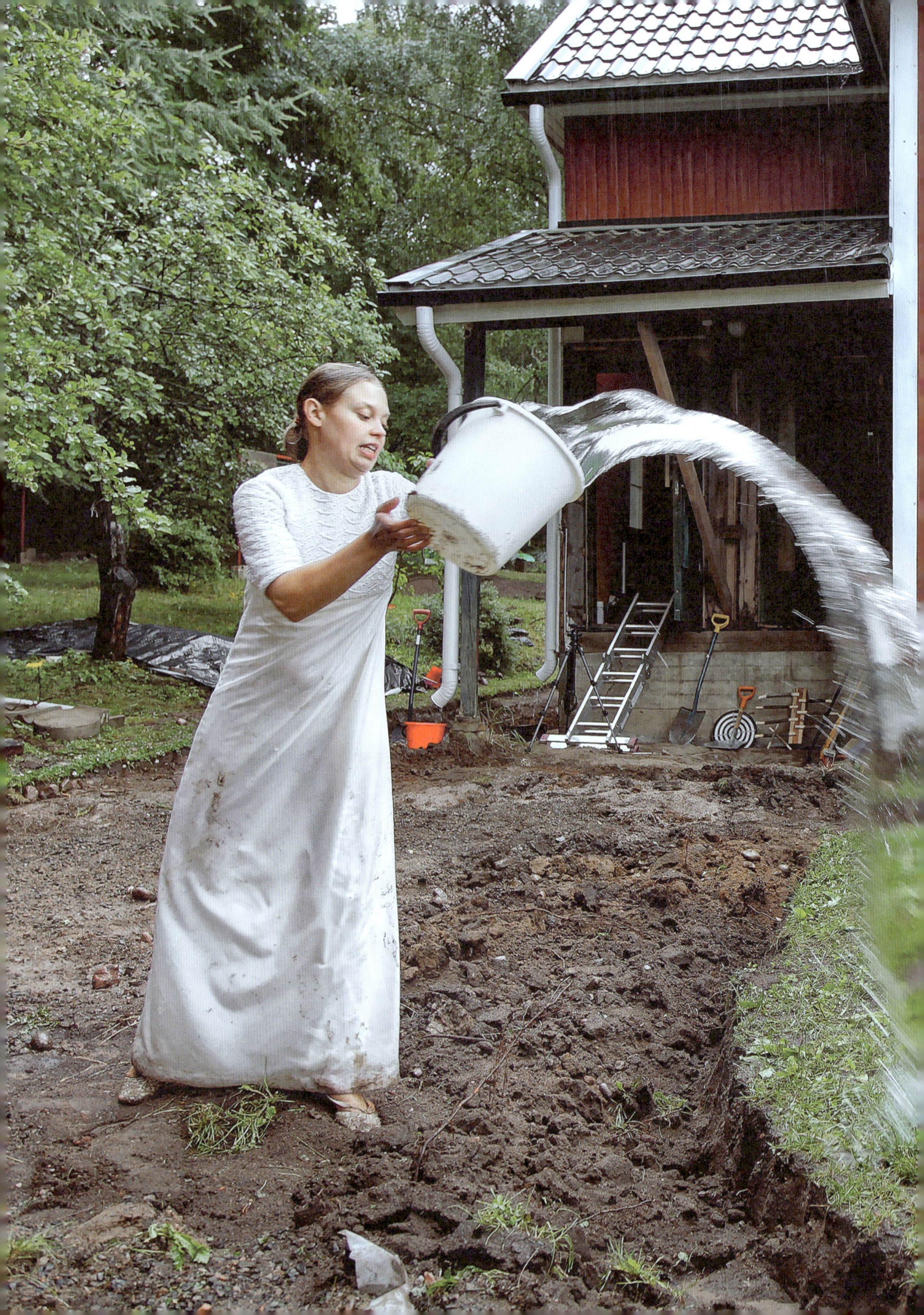

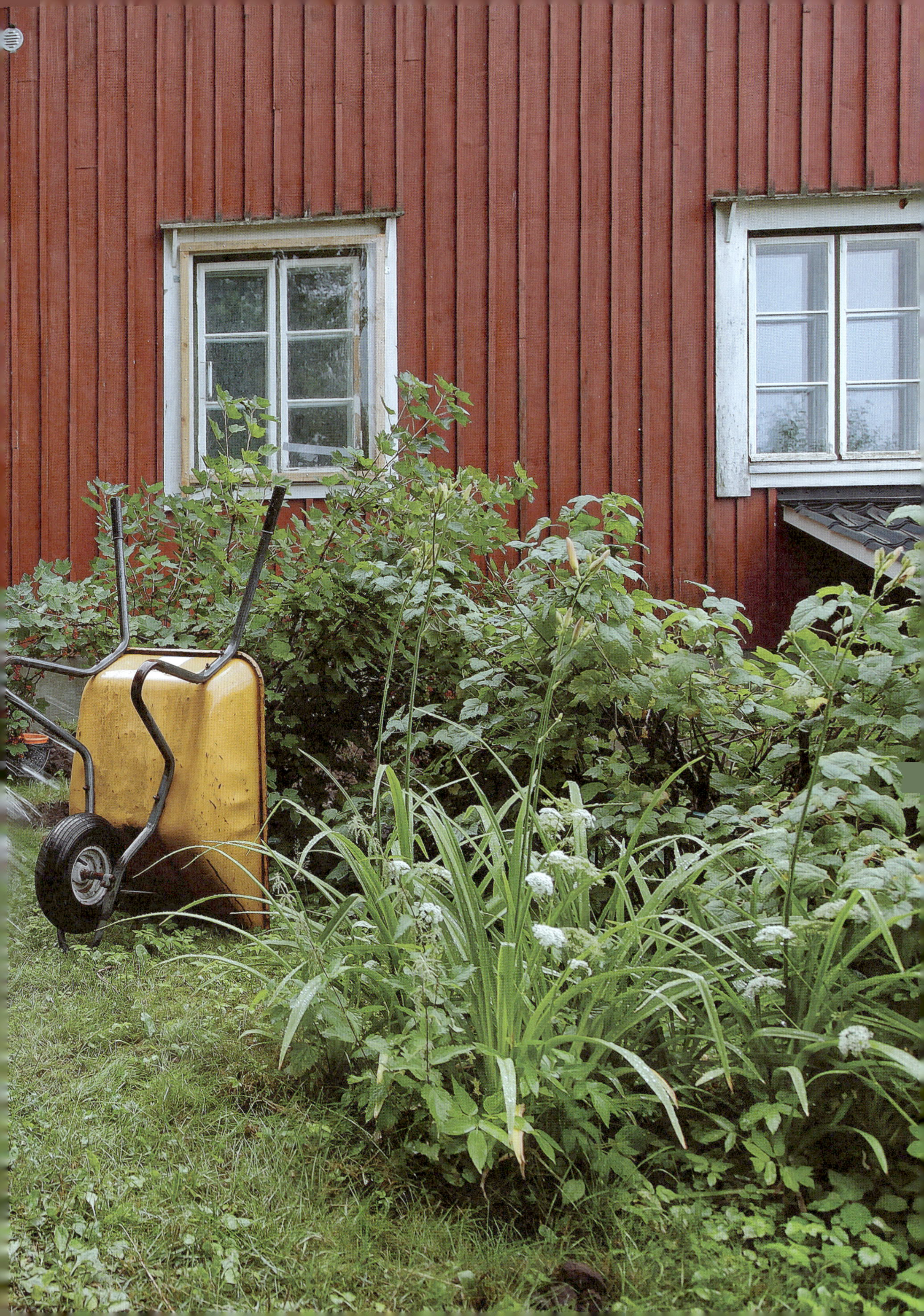

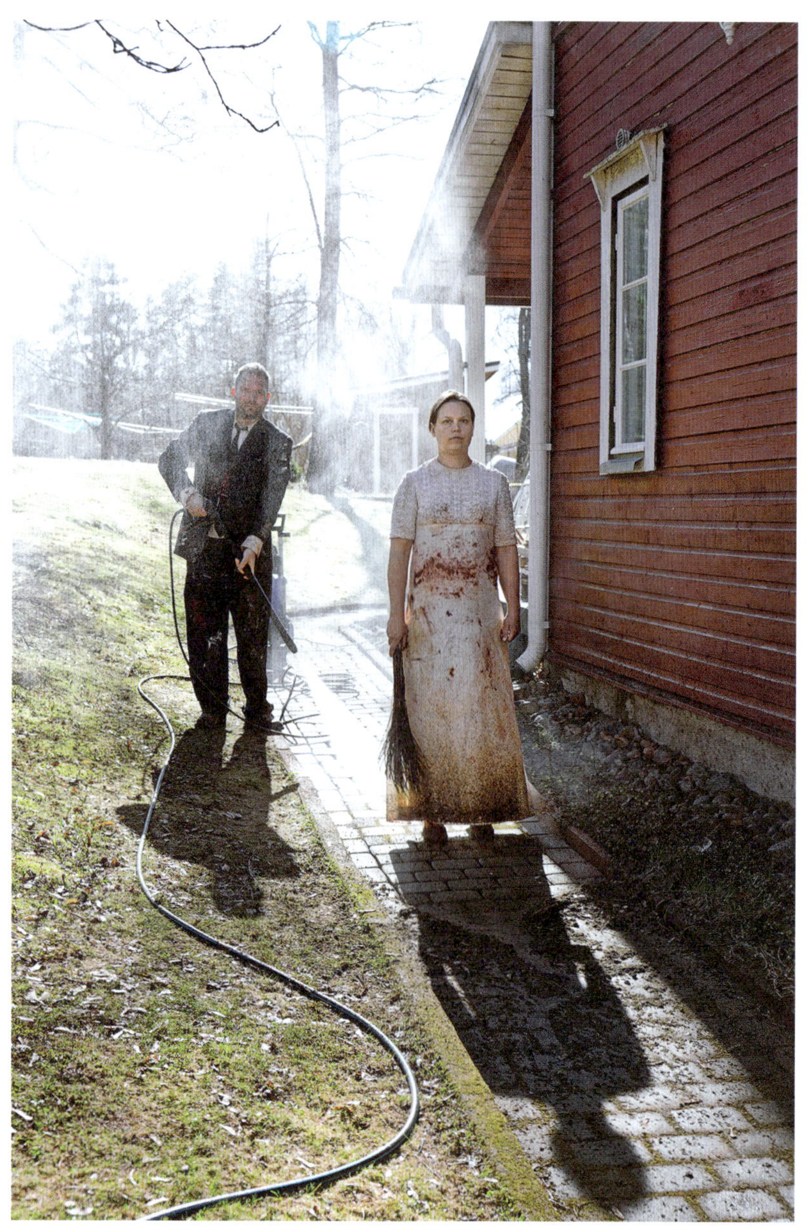

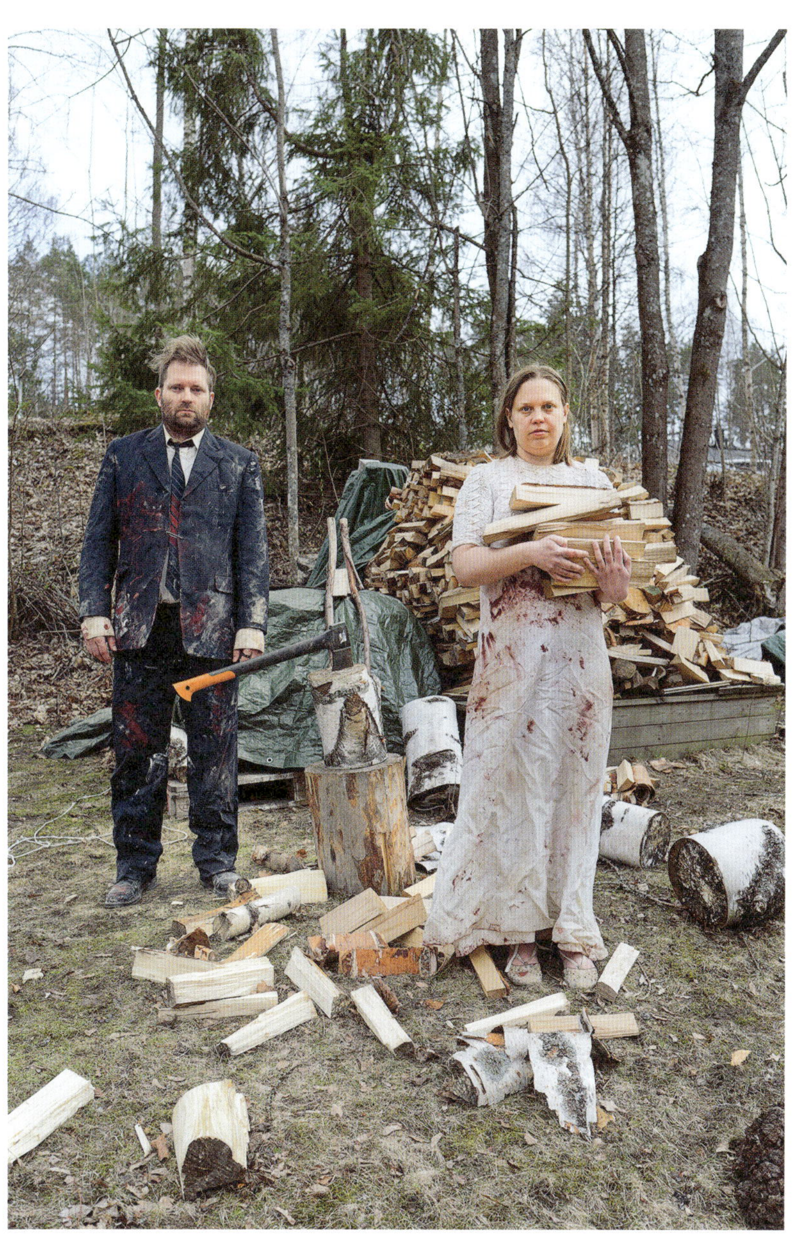

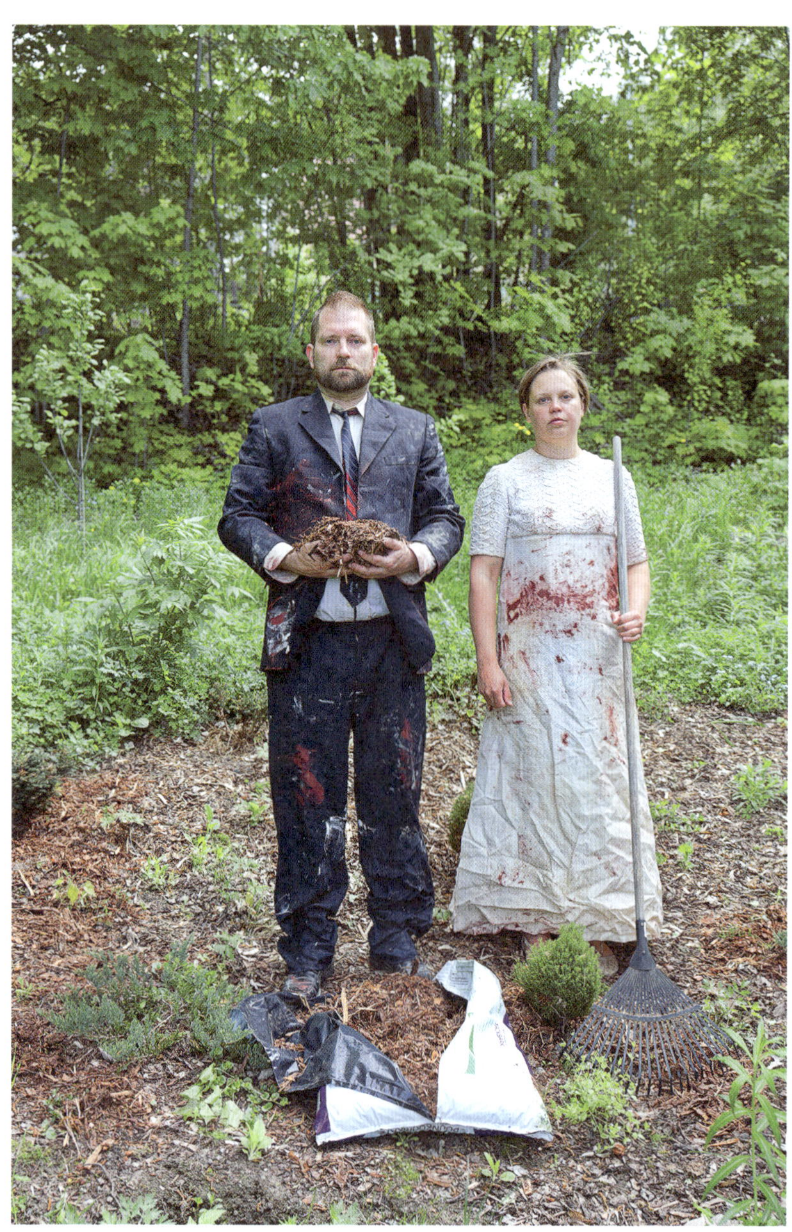

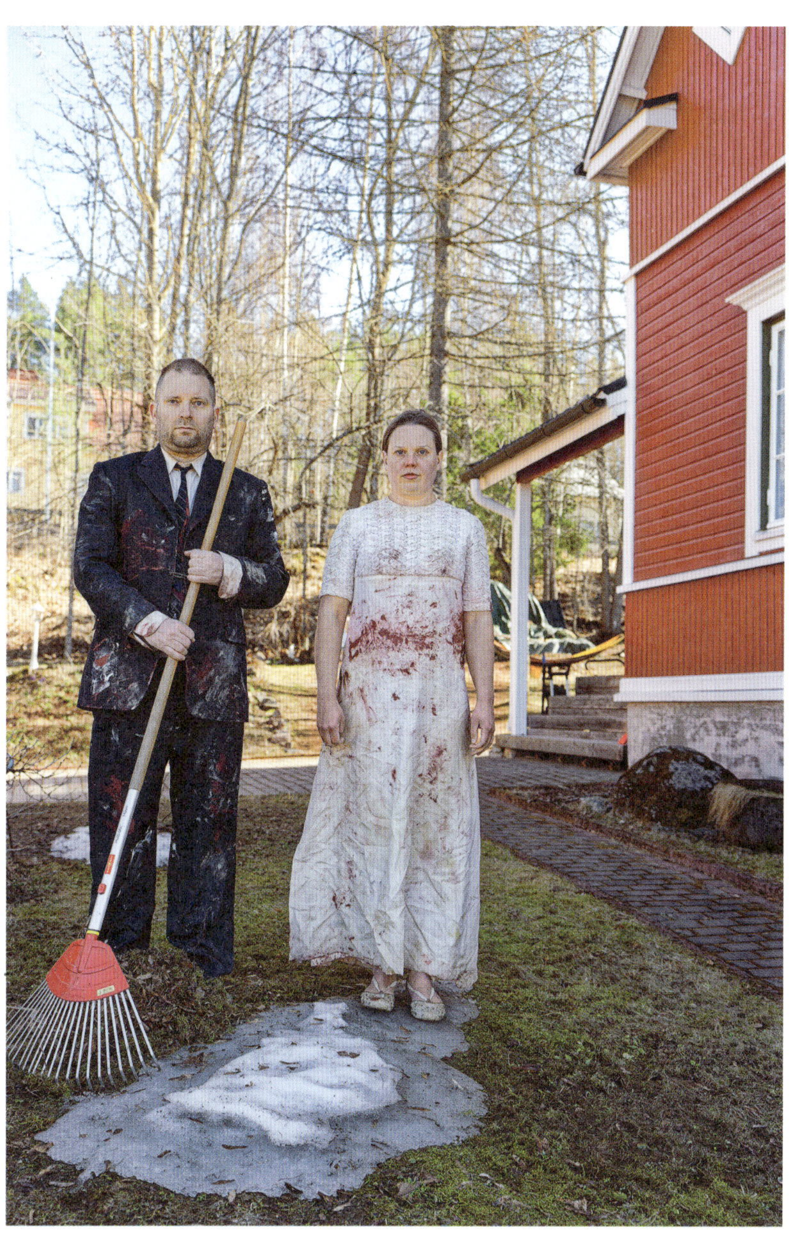

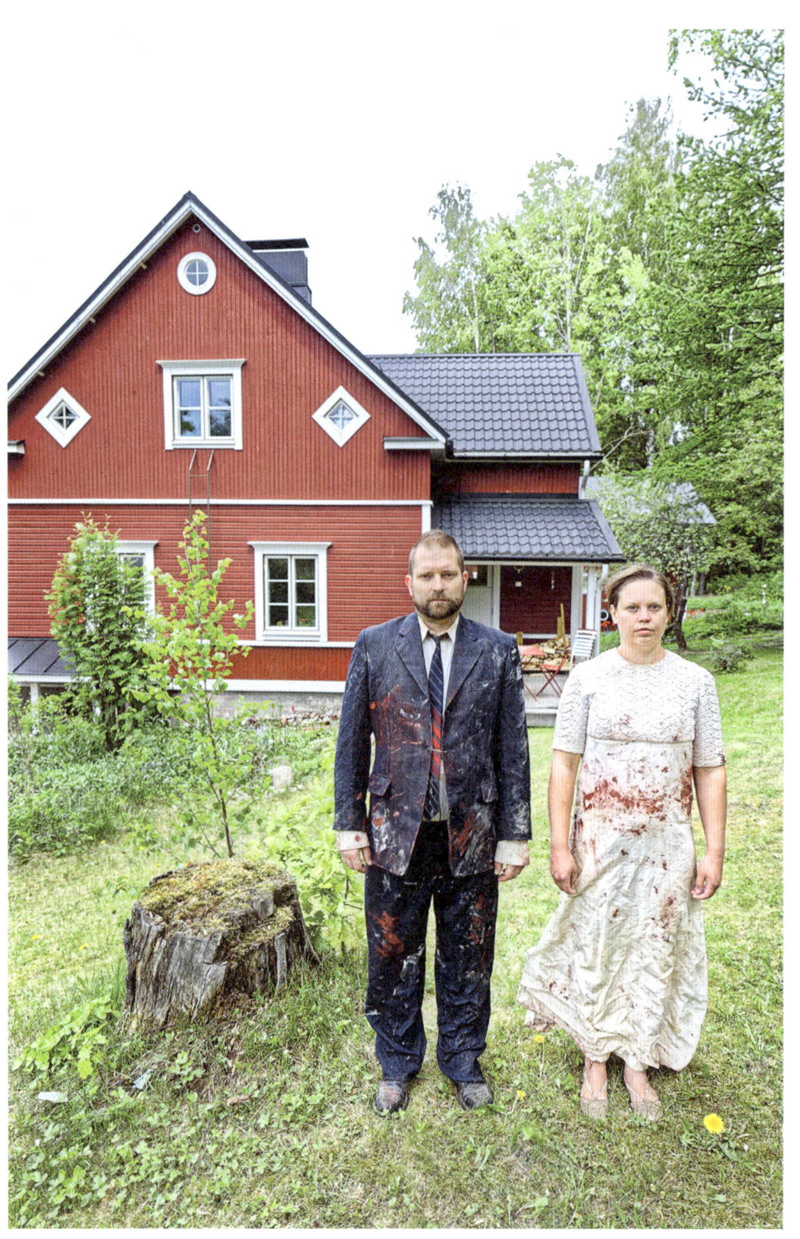

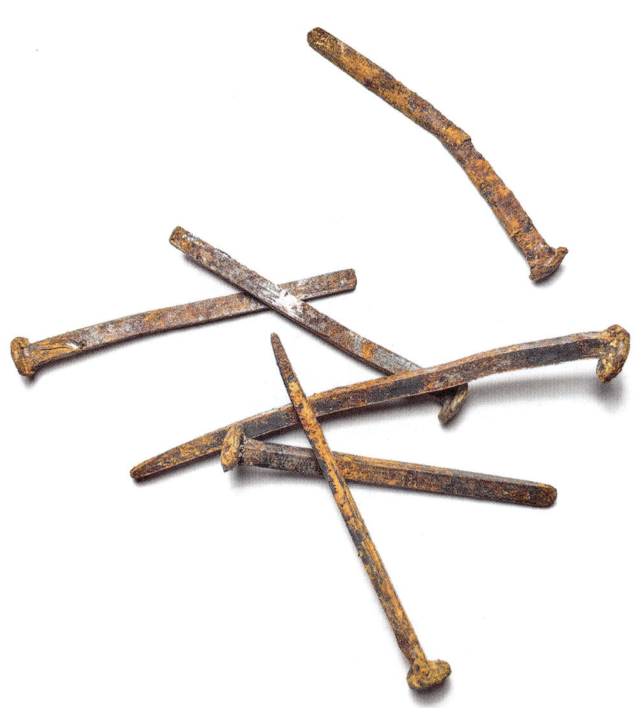

Love *Bears All Things*   Maaretta Jaukkuri

Artists Mammu and Pasi Rauhala are a married couple. Pasi specializes
in new media while Mammu works in theatre and various media. Pasi
says that their different orientations are a source of mutual inspiration.

Bears All Things is a suite of photographs that takes its title from
the apostle Paul's first letter to the Corinthians in the New Testament,
which is renowned as a profound analysis of the essence of love.

So far, this suite consists of over 40 double portraits taken in and around
a building project that the couple started in 2013 and are still working on
today. The suite depicts scenes from the couple's daily life and their years of
renovating an old house and building a new studio. (The dimensions of
the framed images are 64 x 47 cm.)

·

The first image shows a tender moment, apparently depicting the couple as
newlyweds. Pasi is sitting and Mammu is standing, leaning her head towards
him. Gradually, a certain posture begins to recur in the photographs. The couple
stands stiffly, close to each other, looking sternly straight into the camera,
giving the impression that they are concentrating on their inner lives.
In the images, Pasi usually stands on Mammu's left side. Throughout the suite,
the passage of time is documented in the varying lengths of Pasi's hair as well
as in micro changes in their serious faces.

The couple wear their original wedding outfits in every picture.
The garments begin to look dirtier and shabbier as the building project
advances. Red smudges appear on Mammu's white wedding dress – evidently
stains from painting the outer walls of the house. There are various white
stains on Pasi's outfit, and their number and sizes increase with the passing
years. We see the couple clearing, building, raking leaves, ploughing snow,
and engaging in various other seasonal outdoor activities.

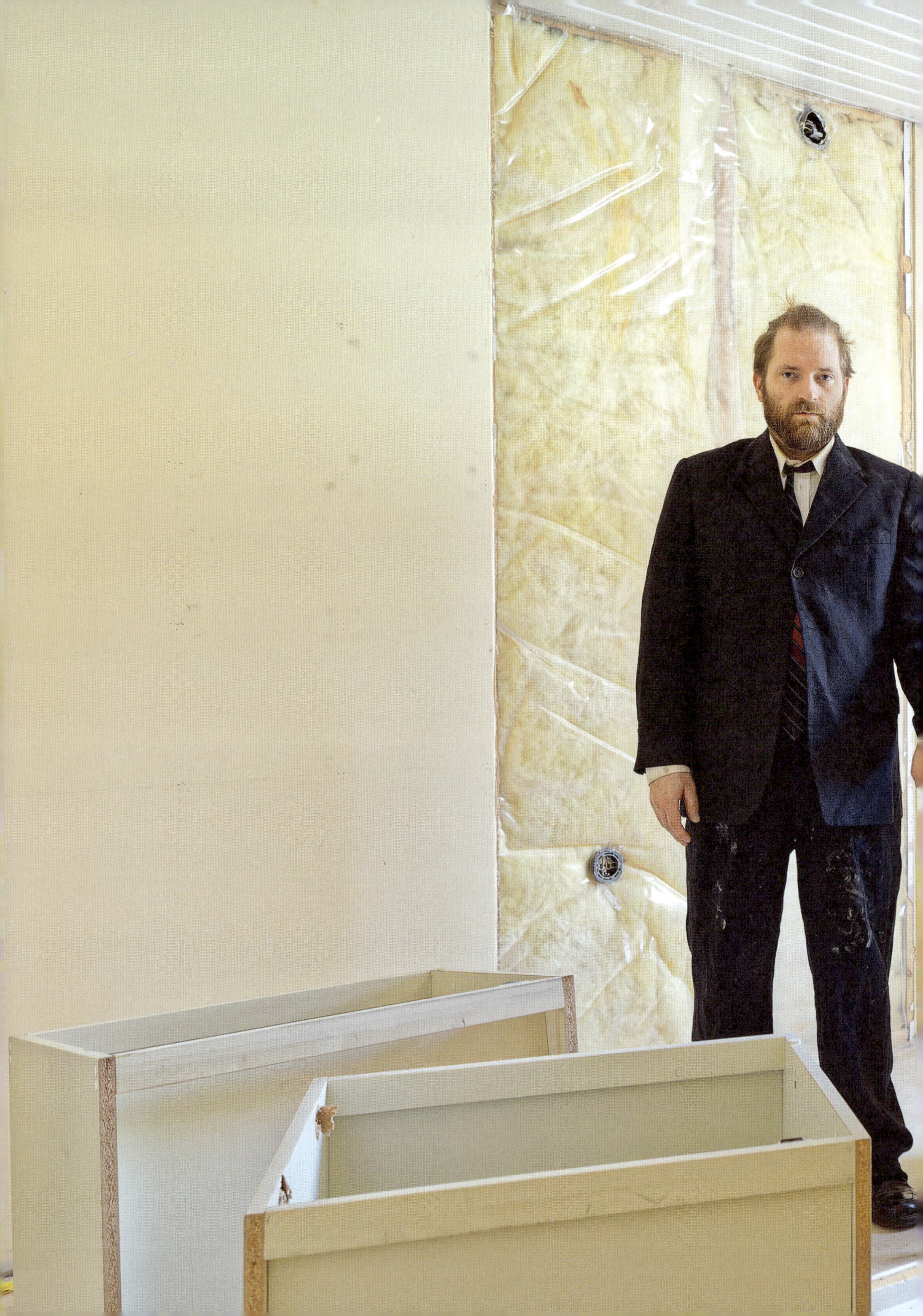

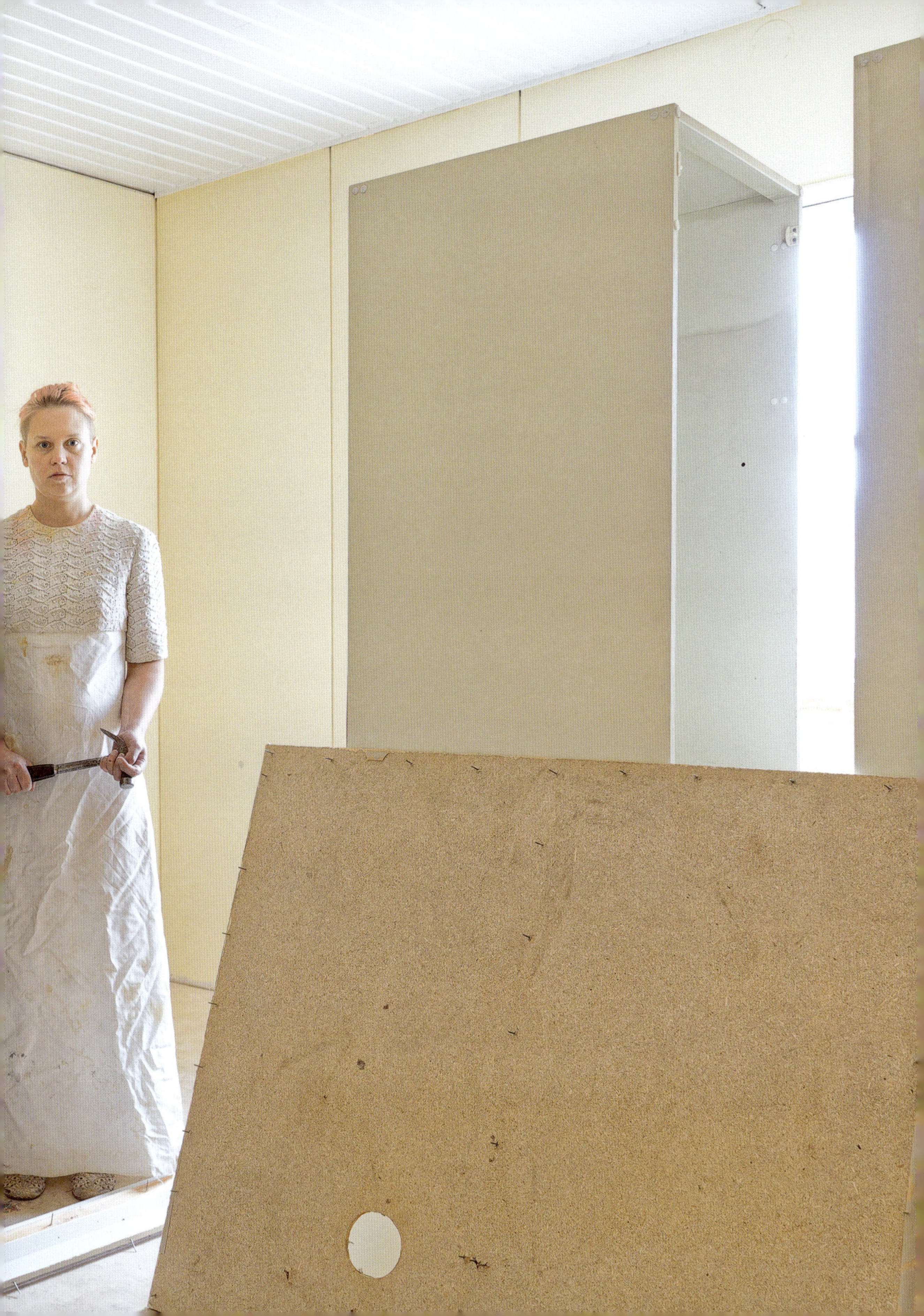

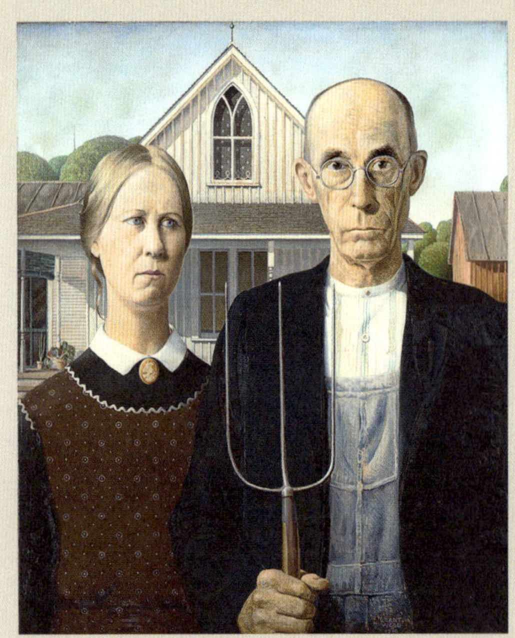

American Gothic
Grant Wood
1930

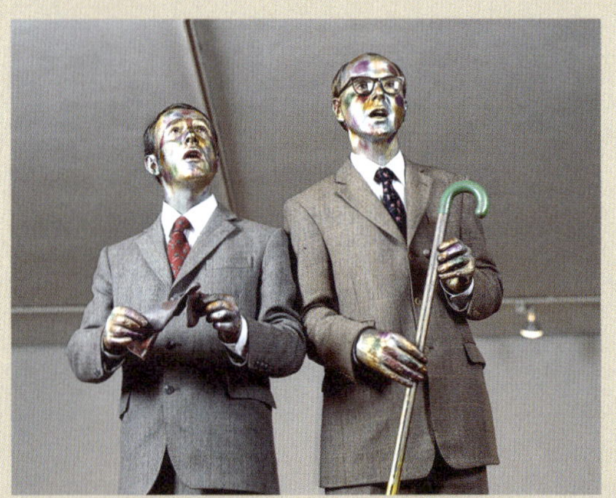

Singing Sculpture
Gilbert & George
1991

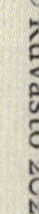

..

When I first saw these images, they reminded me of American Gothic, a double
portrait painted in 1930 by Grant Wood (1891—1942). The stern-looking couple
is dressed in their Sunday best, registering full awareness of being portrayed
in front of their Gothic-inspired wooden home. The man is looking straight
ahead and holding a pitchfork in his hand. With her gaze cast sideways, the
woman seems to be lost in her own thoughts, while the overall atmosphere is
imbued with a kind of single-mindedness. There seems to be no communication
between the pair. The scene and the cultural attributes tell us about their social
roles and the era they are living in. The painting represents a specific epoch of
Regionalism and is today one of the best-known paintings in the US.

   Conscious posing is part of the tradition of portraiture, as too are references
to the model's social status and prominence. Often, the model's personal interests
are suggested through certain symbolic elements.
This tradition continued in early photographic portraits, although photographic portraits and portraiture in general have both closely resonated with key
movements in contemporary art. Issues of identity — both of the artist and the
model — as expressed through ethnicity, sexual orientation, or genre, have been
central to portraiture over the last few decades.

   An early example is the concept of "living sculptures" by the English artist
duo Gilbert and George, who in their photographic works transform portraiture
into role play. Their work still reflects on the identity of me/us, but now understood as something complex and volatile.

   The whole concept of the portrait finds an expanded form in Tracey
Emin's tent work *Everyone I have ever slept with 1963—1995* (1995). Instead of
being a traditional self-portrait, the work consists of a tent containing lists,
descriptions, and mementoes of all the people with whom the artist has shared
her bed during the given period. In this way, the artist shares something about
her life through things and events that have contributed to shaping her identity.

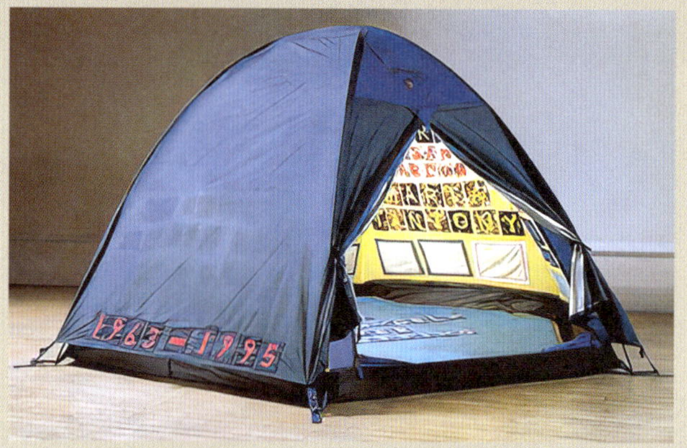

Everyone I have ever slept with 1963–1995
Tracey Emin
1995

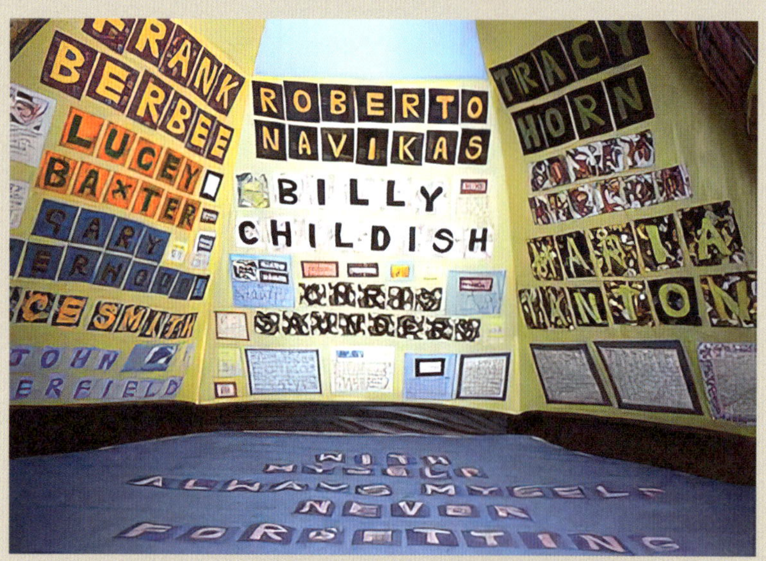

Everyone I have ever slept with 1963–1995
Tracey Emin
1995

The traditional image or icon of portraiture is no longer the signifying
element in this work. Instead, we see a hybrid of a readymade and
an installation. The image — in this case, a self-portrait of the artist —
is conveyed not as an icon, but as index, or by the indexical significance
of the physical environment.

...

This is going on also in Mammu and Pasi's pictures. They are portrayed
in the pictures, but the emphasis is on many years of toil in what feels like
a never-ending project of clearing, pulling down, digging, planning, building,
painting, and using machines both big and small. The fruits of their labour
are hardly ever visible, except in special spaces and situations such as
the seat of the newly repaired water closet being lifted into place.

Generally, one could say that the pictures bear a certain resemblance to
the massive building scenes of socialist realism, which similarly depict work
both ongoing and already completed, thus clearly manifesting an awareness of
the long haul. This is evoked, for instance, by the heavy piles of sharp-edged
boulders, the ultimate purpose of which we viewers can only speculate about.
Pondering this, however, is not the actual point. The signification of this suite
of images seems to relate to time intertwined with the theme of love bearing all
things — a sense of endurance that is ritually reiterated picture after picture.

The 1960s saw the birth of performance art as we understand it today,
which has exerted a major influence both in art and theatre. Performance is
body-oriented art, generally being conceived around a concept or an idea and
expressed by dramatic methods and suggestive props suited for the occasion.

The present suite of pictures, in its particulars, carries on this legacy.
It depicts love that was solidified in a religious ceremony in which the artists
wore traditional wedding attire: she a white frock and he a dark suit. During
the ceremony, Paul's letter to the Corinthians was read aloud, including the
reference to love bearing all things. The suite does not contain a picture of
the actual wedding ceremony. The line bears all things has become a memory,
and its vital message is ritually actualized time after time in this series. This
lies at the heart or core of the work.

To keep this important message in mind amid the hurried pace of daily
life and the chaos of clearing and building, the couple decided to keep on
photographing themselves wearing their wedding outfits in various physically
and psychologically challenging daily situations. This process could be defined as
a psychological ritual during which the wedding pledge is repeatedly reaffirmed.

Throughout the over eleven years of working on this series — which is still
ongoing — the common element is the performative presence of the couple, their
rigid posture being perfectly matched by their sincere yet determined demeanour.
Their presence connects all the images in the series, thus functioning as a kind of
reflective surface for the situations around them. In no way do they react to the
chaos surrounding them, but instead they seem to be concentrating on their inner
worlds and shared vows. The meaning is created virtually by mental images, as it
is not directly expressed in the picture, nor in the milieu or the portrayed persons.
Instead, signification is assigned in the minds of the viewers. Virtuality
is a central concept in the analysis of seeing, both in photography and film.

Art or photography that is based on index instead of icon is often exemplified
by a footprint in sand telling us that someone has been walking on the beach.
The physical presence of building materials, machines and tools inform us that
demolition and building has been completed and is also ongoing and forthcoming.
A house is being partially pulled down, repaired and reconstructed.

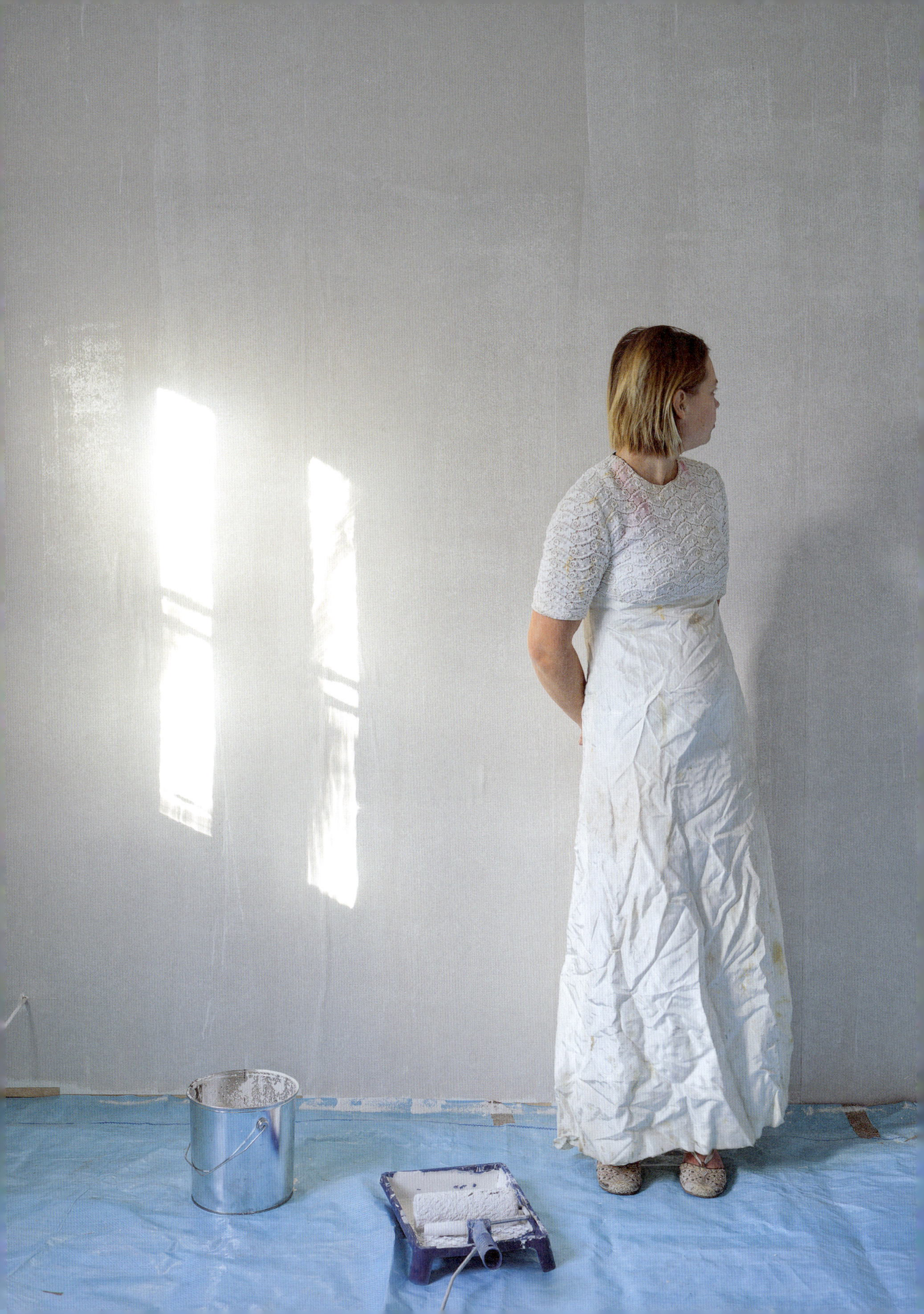

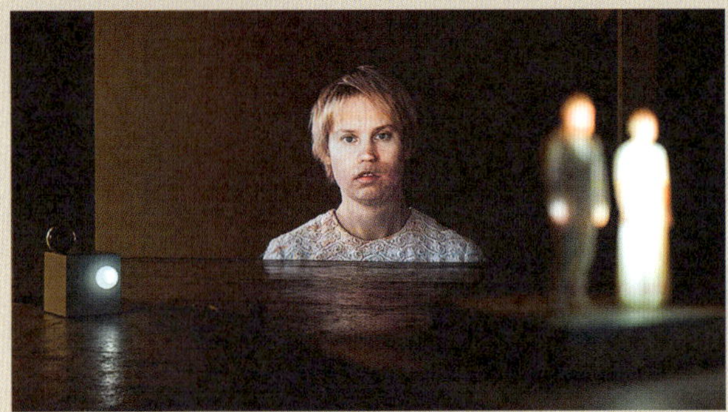

What is in Part Disappears
Mammu & Pasi Rauhala
Huuto Gallery,
2016

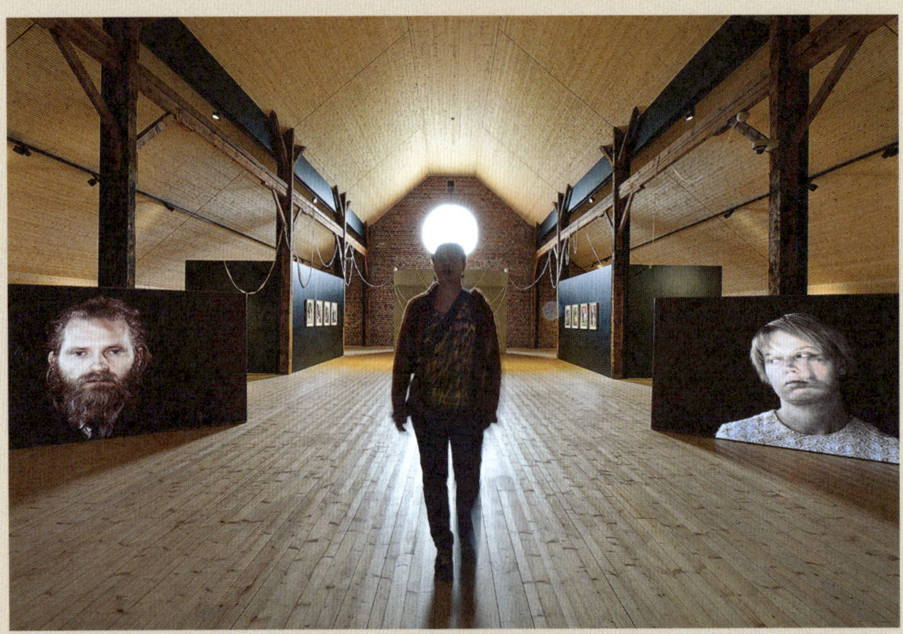

What is in Part Disappears
Mammu & Pasi Rauhala
Seinäjoki Art Hall,
2022

The storyline in the images is built upon singular situations. The variations establish each photograph as an independent artwork, but when shown as a series, they spin a story. The viewer understands the challenges captured in each scene — indeed the building project does not seem to proceed anywhere... or does it? We do not know what takes place in between the pictures, or when they were taken, as the only references to the passing of time are the changing scenes and seasons and the increasing number of stains on the ever-shabbier clothes. The virtual storyline is left for the viewer to narrate in their mind, where the still images gel together into a film-like story. We use mental pictures to fill in the gaps and intervals, thus creating a plot and postulating a story of what has been and is going on. Our mental images start connecting with the viewed optical images.

Sutton, Damian. 2009. *Photography, Cinema, Memory: The Crystal Image of Time*, (p. 44). Sutton is here quoting Gilles Deleuze's Cinema 2: Time-Image.

What happens in our minds is that "The actual optical image crystallizes with its own virtual image..."(Sutton, 2009) The result is, then, a crystal-image. Crystal-images cannot be halted, instead they keep on creating new images that fluctuate between the seen optical and virtually created mental images. Thus, a narrative is born in the mind of the viewer based both on the individual images and the entire suite.

Further expanding on the themes of the photographic series, the artists have made the video *What is in Part Disappears* (2016) and an ensemble of small sculptures titled *Hanging in There* (2019). Both these works further explore and deepen the emotional thrust of the photographic work.

The video *What is in Part Disappears* is a reflection on the themes of symbiosis and separateness as described in the Bible. It also reflects on how in, long-standing relationships, the partners mutually imitate and adopt each other's reactions and behaviour. These responses are triggered by "mirror neurons" in a process that is currently being researched in the neurosciences. By projecting their portraits on top of the other, Mammu's face on Pasi's, and vice versa, the artists blend

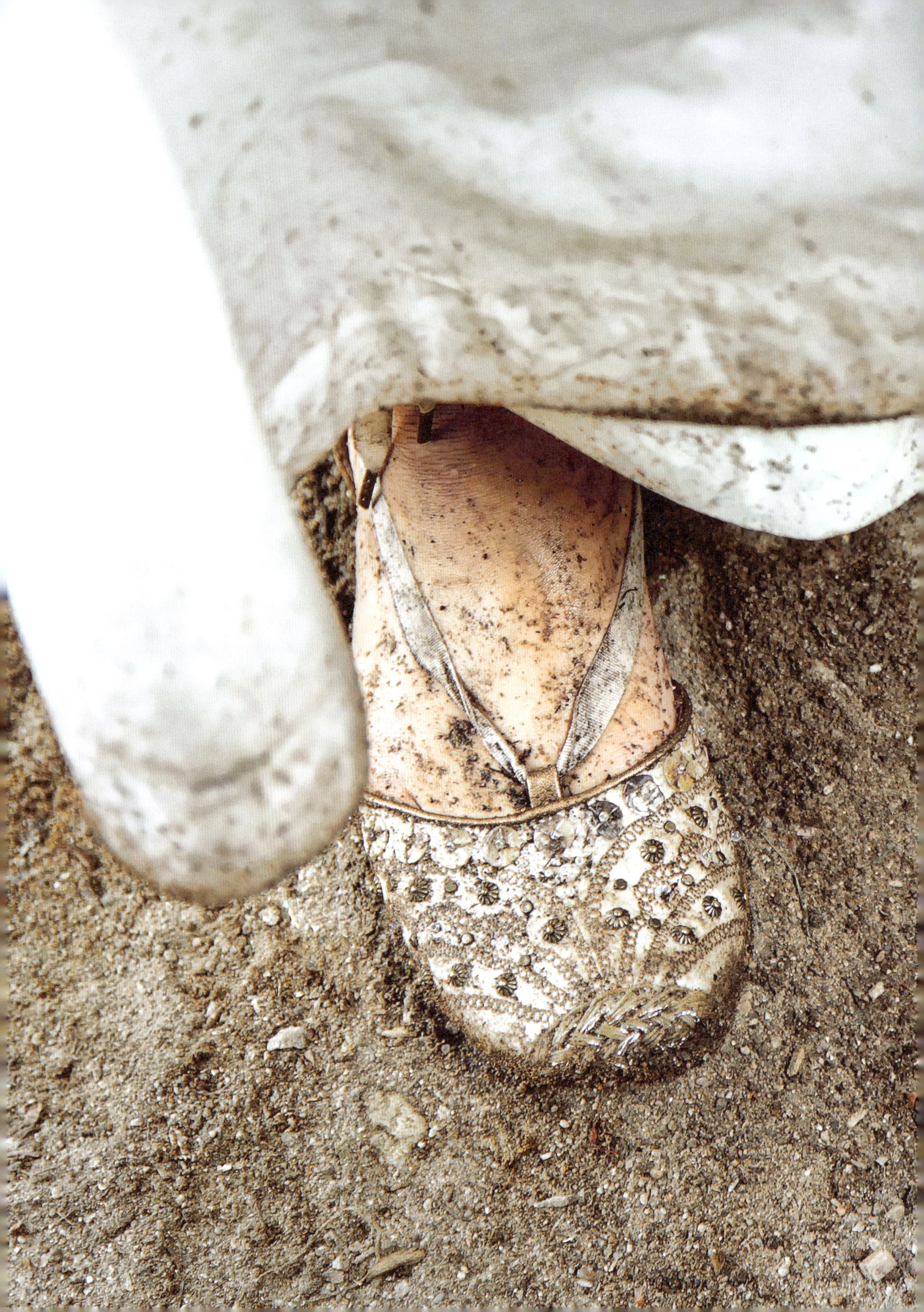

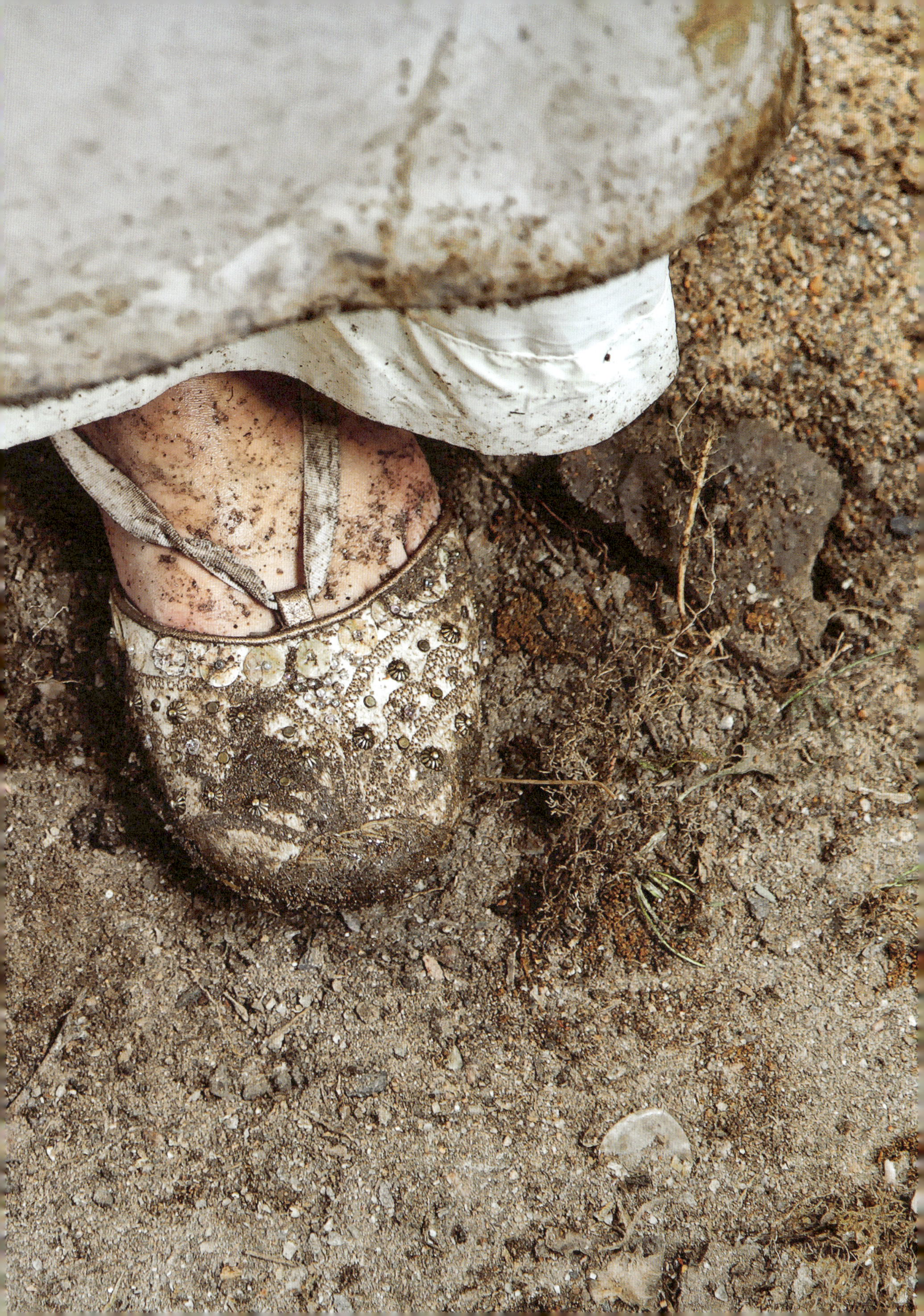

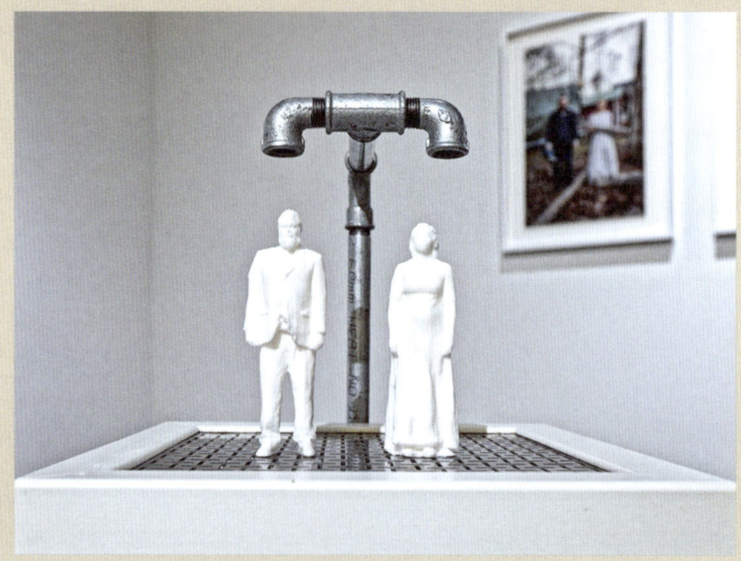

Hanging in There (soap)
Mammu & Pasi Rauhala
2019

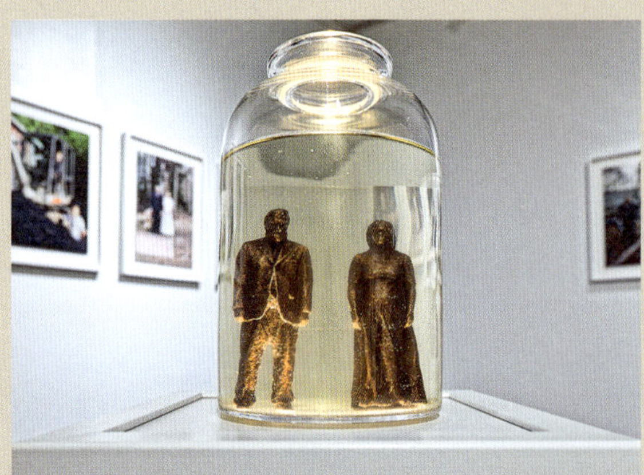

Hanging in There (bronze)
Mammu & Pasi Rauhala
2019

masculine and feminine characteristics in a kind of gender-bending, morphed two-in-one portrait. One could perhaps say that the overlapping video portraits form a kind of technically produced version of crystal-images. The mental process of crystallisation, however, continues also with these images in the spectator's mind.

The group of three statuettes in *Hanging in There* incorporates ephemeral materials such as living organisms and bacteria. The scene consists of three small sculptures of wedding couples, their physical shape and appearance being subject to change under the altering exhibition conditions. One of the couples is cast in soap and placed under a running water faucet. In this series, too, the spectator's responses to images, situations and conditions give rise to mental images.

. . . .

Time and its influence on our lives seems to be a central theme in the art of Mammu and Pasi Rauhala. There are things we wish would never change, but they inevitably still do, like everything else in life. The artists have decided that the one thing that will never change is the promise they made to each other — it will be kept alive irrespective of the conditions they face. To remind themselves of this, they keep on performing their joint ritual. A ritual is loosely defined as a performance in which the details are always faithfully repeated. In this suite of photographs, video and the statuettes alike, the artists have found ways to capture the passage of time, its challenges, as well as the promise they made to each other. Everything around them will inevitably change, but their promise is not made of a changeable substance. It will be kept.

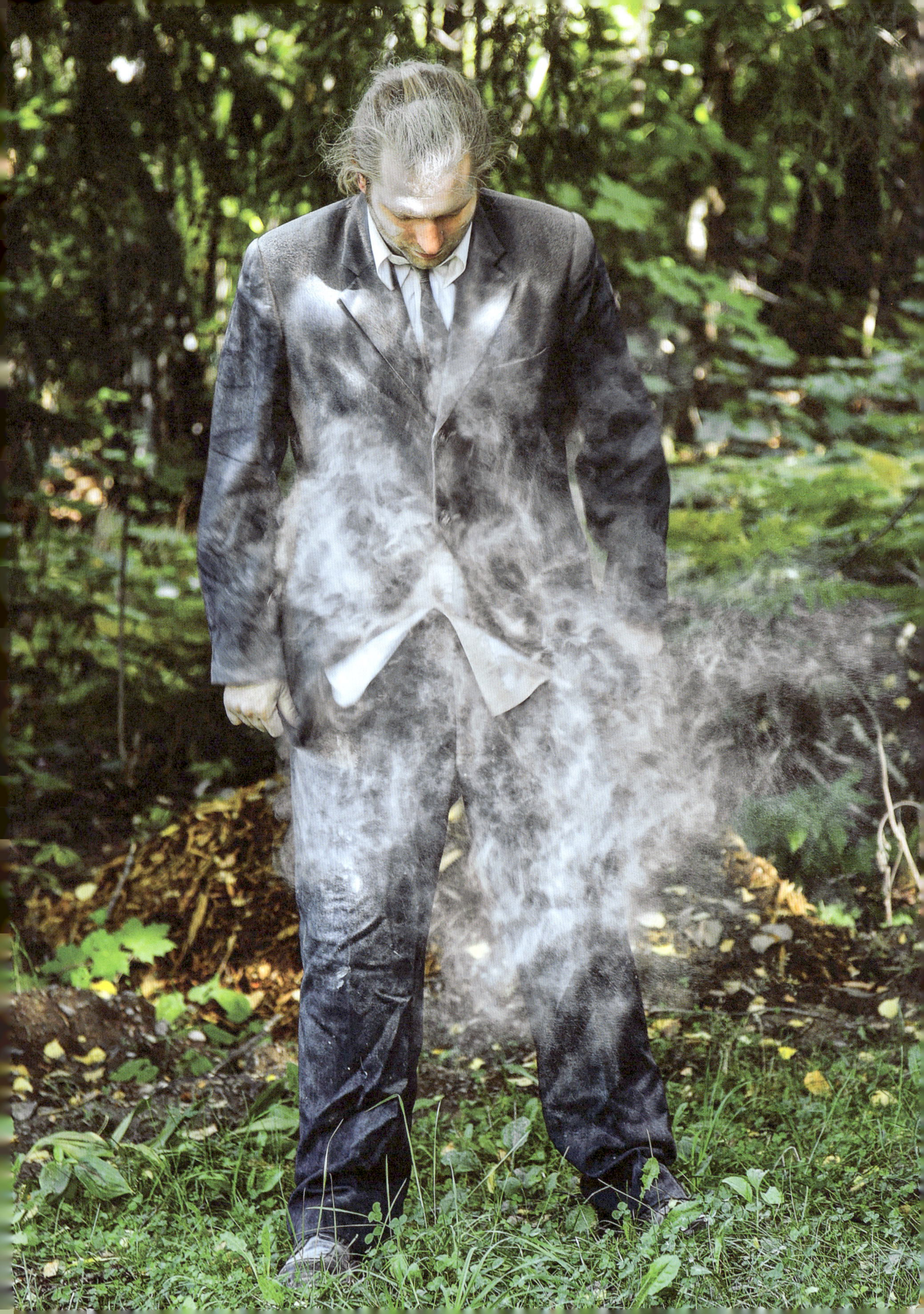

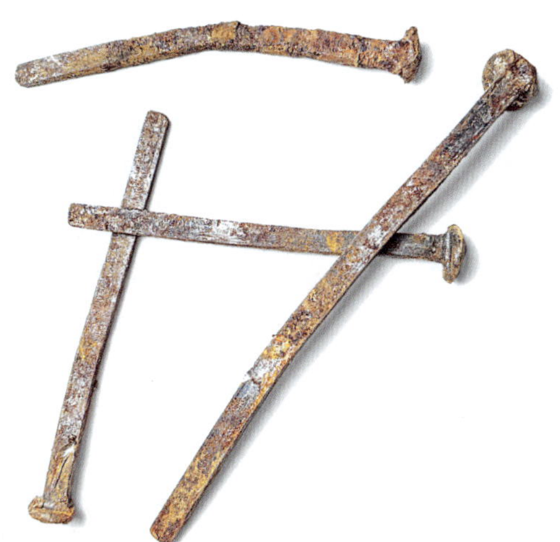

Epiloque

Thank you everyone who has taken part in this project: Our designer, Ilona, who understood our project and created this beautiful book. Maaretta, who took the time to get to know us and wrote a text that placed our work in the context of art history, a perspective that we could never have achieved on our own. Petri, who is a master of image processing. All our contacts at Kerber Verlag, who believed in this book from the very beginning and supported us throughout the entire process. Eino, our beloved child, who not only lives with us in this old and forever unfinished house, but who has also helped us create this book and our website. Silja and Suvi, who made some final corrections to the text. Thank you to our funders, The Arts Promotion Centre Finland and Frame Contemporary Art Finland.

Last but not least, thanks to the friends and family who have helped us with the house throughout the years. Not everything is done by ourselves, but also with the help of a community. Much love to all.

Even though the book is now finished, the renovations and other work around the house continue. Perhaps it's time to fix the roof next? Our world is facing many changes and challenges, so is the house. Time goes by but the house stands steadfast providing us shelter, a place we call home.

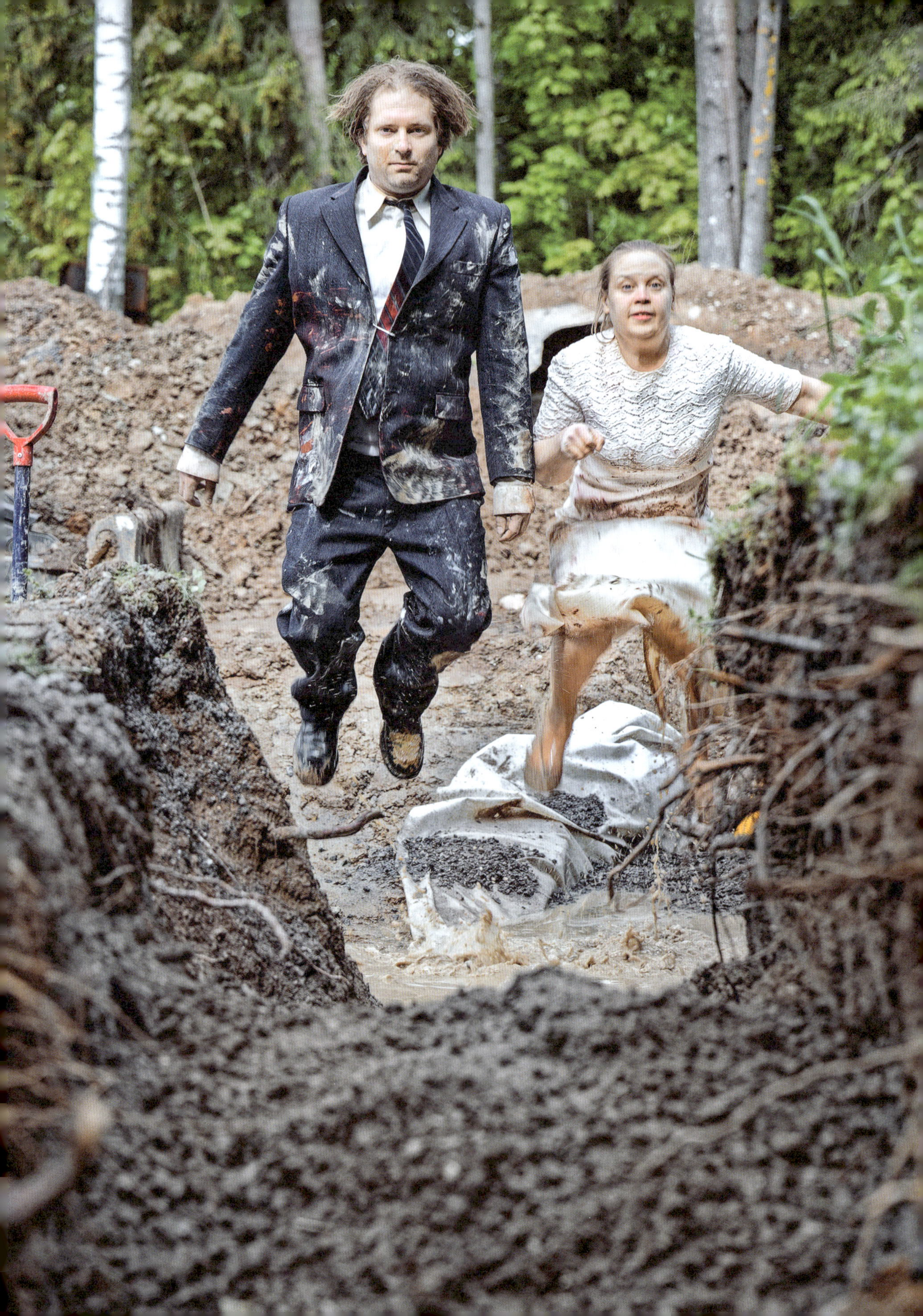

Biography

Mammu and Pasi Rauhala have been collaboratively creating artwork since 2010, weaving their talents into a harmonious partnership. The heartbeat of their creative journey is *Bears All Things*, a transformative project that has captured their focus since 2013.

Residing and operating as an inseparable duo, Mammu and Pasi thrive in a world where their lives and work intertwine, seamlessly contributing to each other's artistic processes. Their existence revolves around shared brainstorming sessions, the rhythmic exchange of ideas, and the art of assisting one another. From the inception of their collaborative efforts, they've embraced the essence of synergy, harnessing their unique strengths to craft works that resonate beyond their individual capabilities. Together, they've come up with creations that neither could have conceived without the other—a testament to the power of their partnership.

Mammu Rauhala holds a Bachelor of Culture and Arts degree in theatre. All through her life, she has used both the visual arts and her body to express herself. Mammu's practice experiments with, and straddles the intersections of, sculpture, painting, media art, and performance, among other things. Art masks and related performances are the objects of her passion. Mammu has worked as a drama teacher, a director, and a coordinator of applied arts. In addition, she has participated in numerous activities.

Pasi Rauhala has a Master's degree in Photography from Aalto University, as well as a degree in Time and Space Arts from the Academy of Fine Arts in Helsinki. Pasi is dedicated to the realm of media art, with a specific focus on interactivity, spatial experience, and public environments. With two decades of professional experience, he has been engaged as an educator across major Finnish art schools and has contributed to several art projects, in roles such as artist, curator, producer, and coordinator. For Pasi, the world of art represents an ongoing odyssey, brimming with limitless possibilities and destinations.

Exhibitions

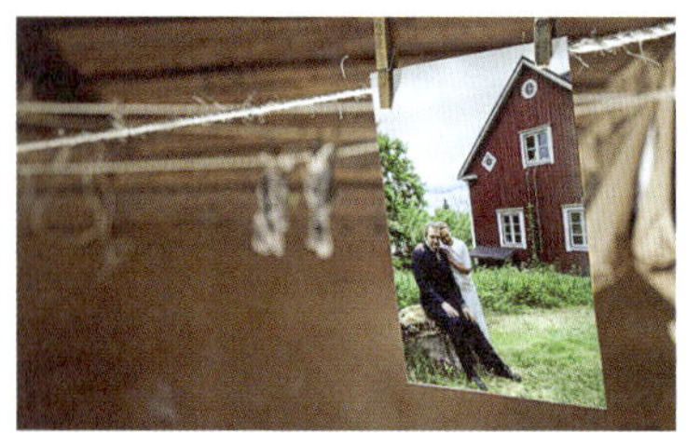

2013
Paikkari Performance Festival
Lohja, Finland
Curator Pekka Kainulainen

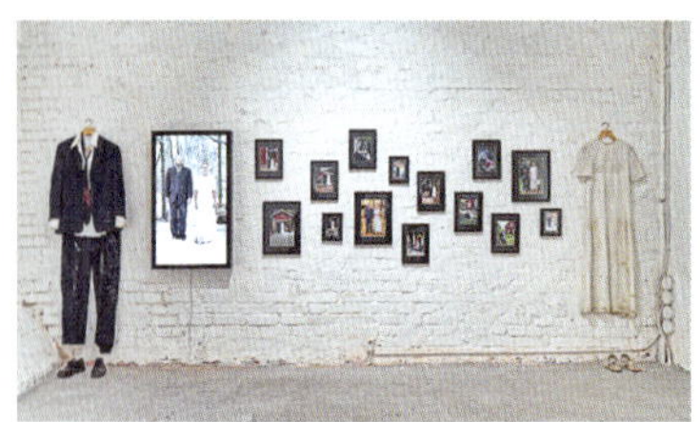

2014
Festen
Galleria Forum Box
Helsinki, Finland

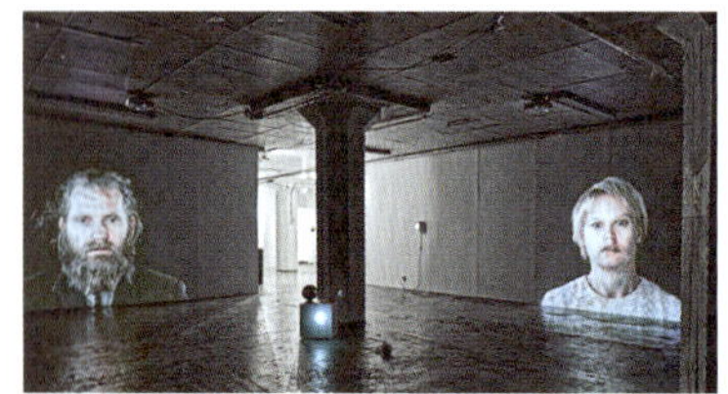

2016
Love Never Fails
Galleria Huuto
Helsinki, Finland

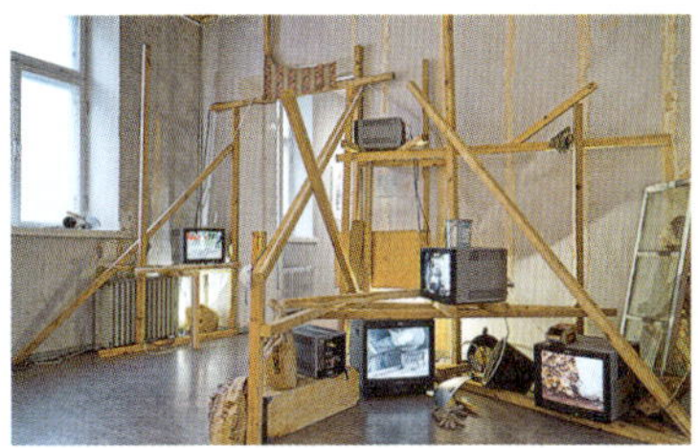

2016
Bears All Things
Galleria Lapinlahti
Helsinki, Finland

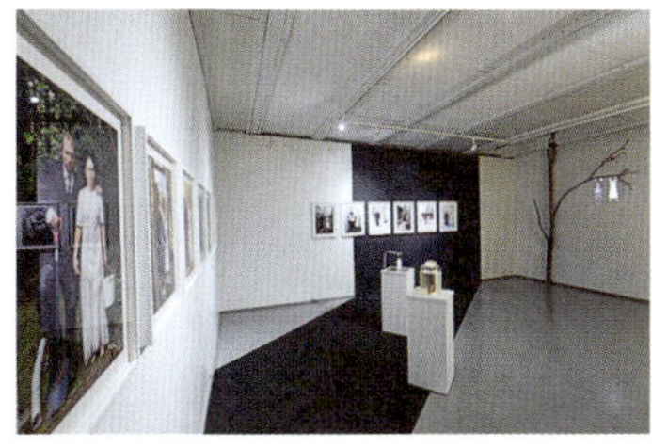

2019
Human Era
Mänttä Art Festival
Mänttä, Finland
Curator Marja Helander

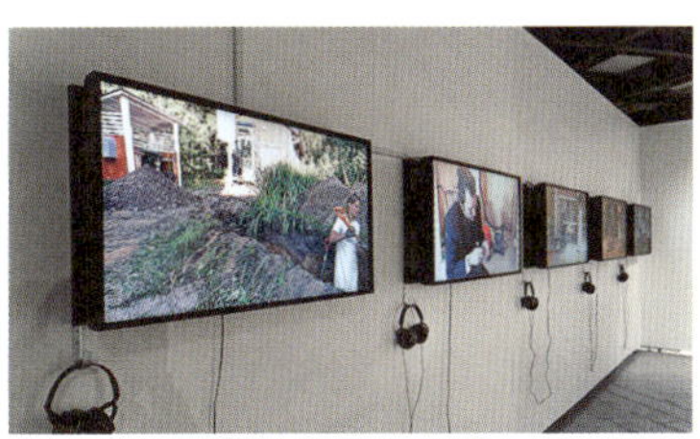

2016
Lost in Archive
Riga Art Space
Riga, Latvia
Curators Inga Lāce and
Andra Silapētere

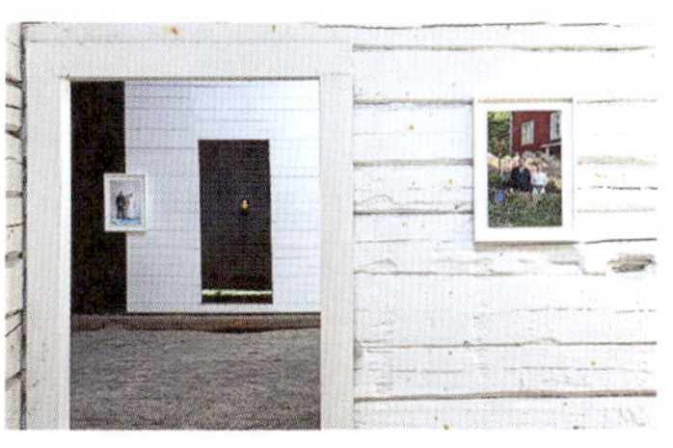

2020
ARS+KÄRSÄMÄKI 2.0
Kärsämäki, Finland
Curators Raisa Raekallio and
Misha del Val

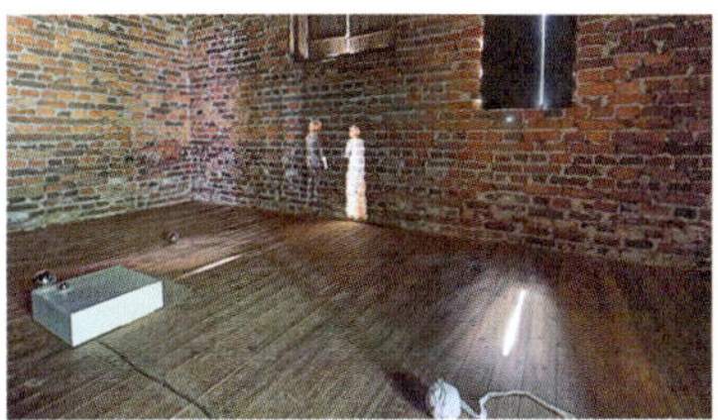

2018
Pyhäniemi 2018
Pyhäniemen kartano
Hollola, Finland
Curator Riikka Latva-Somppi

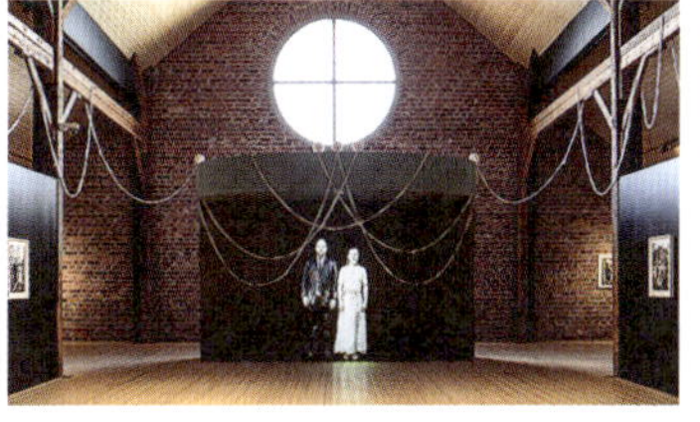

2022
Bears All Things – First 10 years
Seinäjoki Art Hall
Seinäjoki, Finland

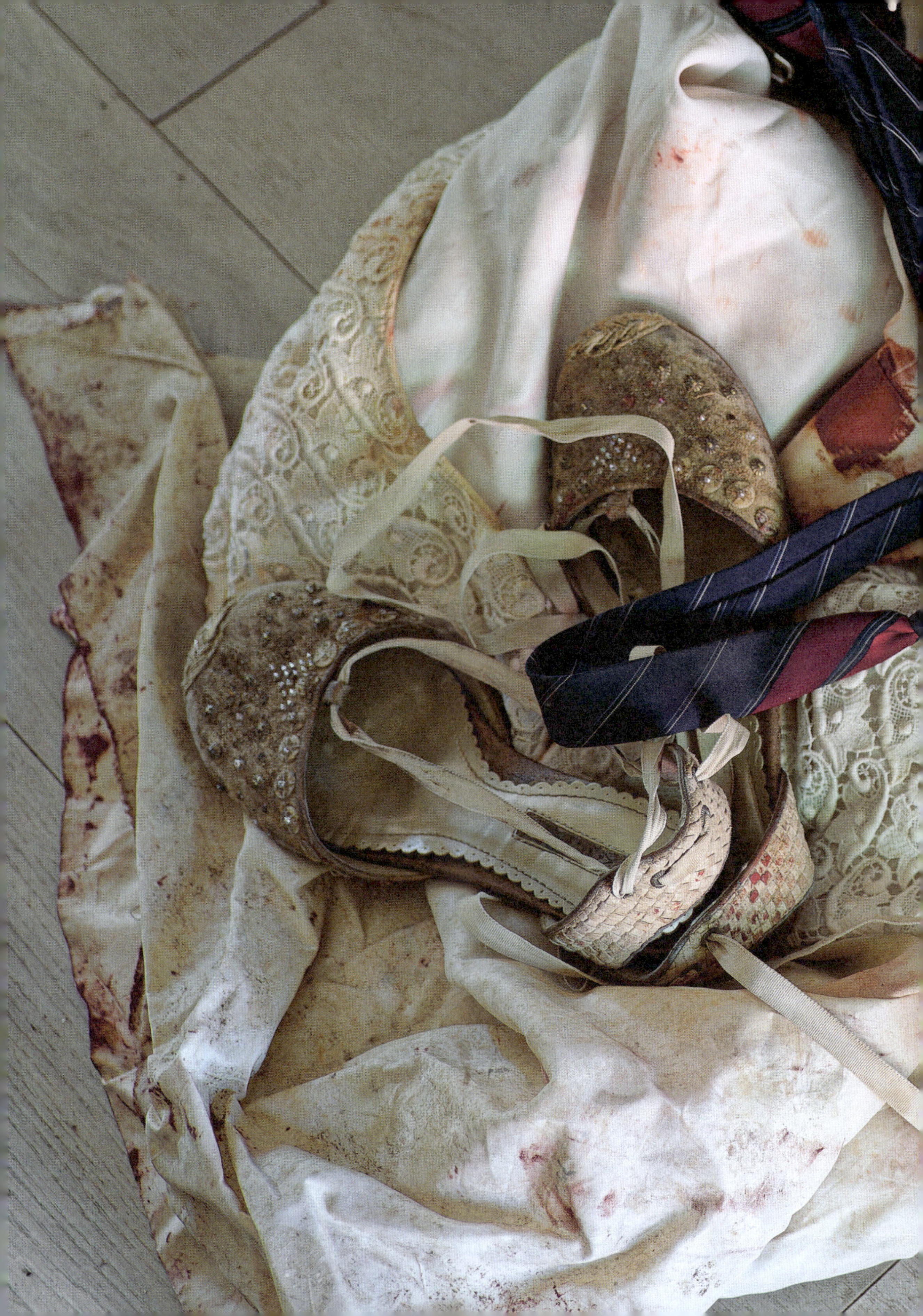

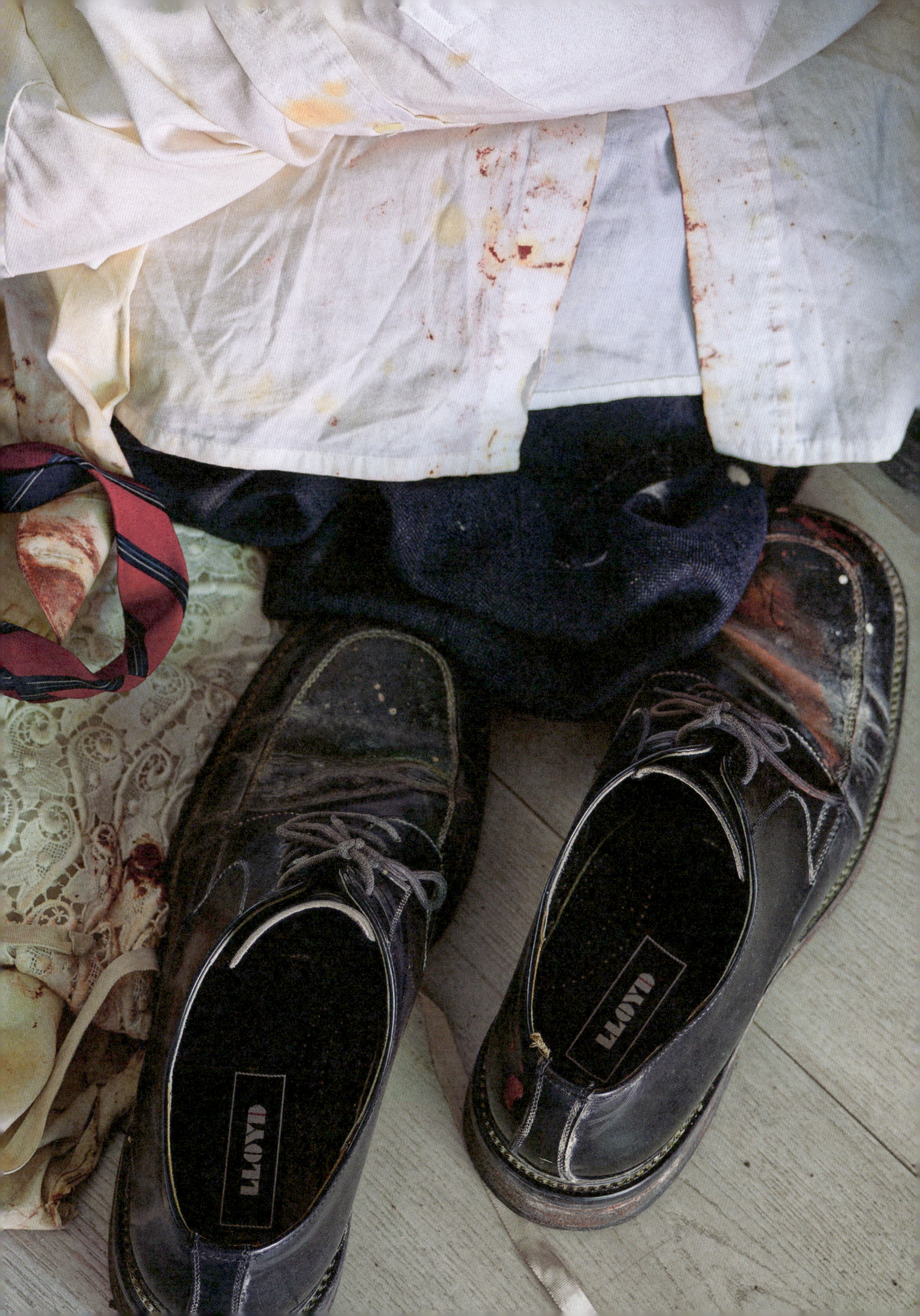
LLOYD
LLOYD

Colophon

Texts Maaretta Jaukkuri, Mammu Rauhala
Design Ilona Ilottu / Dog Design
Proofreading Silja K Creations, Suvi Korpikoski
Image processing Petri Kuokka / Aarnipaja
Project management Lydia Fuchs / Kerber Verlag
Production Jens Bartneck / Kerber Verlag
Papers Munken Lynx 80g/m² & 150g/m²
Font Novela

ISBN 978-3-7356-0967-0
www.kerberverlag.com
Printed in Germany

The Deutsche Nationalbibliothek
lists this publication in the Deutsche
Nationalbibliografie: dnb.de.

Supported by

Taiteen edistämiskeskus
Centret för konstfrämjande
Arts Promotion Centre Finland

www.bearsallthings.art

Kerber Verlag
Detmolder Straße 60
33604 Bielefeld
Germany
+49 521 950 08 10
+49 521 950 08 88 (F)
info@kerberverlag.com
kerberverlag.com

**Kerber publications are
distributed worldwide**

ACC Art Books
Sandy Lane
Old Martlesham
Woodbridge, IP12 4SD
UK
+44 1394 38 99 50
+44 1394 38 99 99 (F)
accartbooks.com
uksales@accartbooks.com

Artbook | D.A.P.
75 Broad Street, Suite 630
New York, NY 10004
USA
+1 (212) 627-1999
+1 (212) 627-9484 (F)
artbook.com
orders@dapinc.com

AVA Verlagsauslieferung AG
Centralweg 16
8910 Affoltern am Albis
Switzerland
+41 44 762 42 50
+41 44 762 42 10 (F)
avainfo@ava.ch

Zeitfracht Medien GmbH
Distribution
+49 711 7860 2254
bestellung@zeitfracht.de

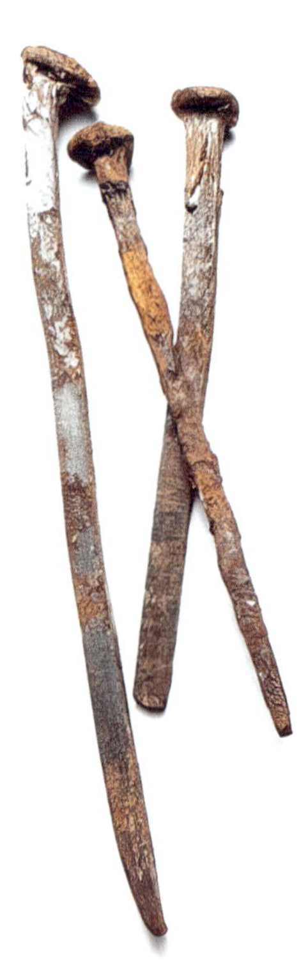